Grammar
Success

4

TEACHER'S GUIDE

Raising Writing Standards

Pie Corbett   Rachel Roberts

OXFORD

OXFORD

UNIVERSITY PRESS

Great Clarendon Street, Oxford OX2 6DP

Oxford University Press is a department of the University of Oxford.
It furthers the University's objective of excellence in research, scholarship,
and education by publishing worldwide in

Oxford New York

Auckland Bangkok Buenos Aires Cape Town Chennai
Dar es Salaam Delhi Hong Kong Istanbul Karachi Kolkata
Kuala Lumpur Madrid Melbourne Mexico City Mumbai Nairobi
São Paulo Shanghai Singapore Taipei Tokyo Toronto

with an associated company in Berlin

Oxford is a registered trade mark of Oxford University Press
in the UK and in certain other countries

British Library Cataloguing in Publication Data

Data available

1 3 5 7 9 10 8 6 4 2

ISBN 019 834 292 6

Designed and produced by Oxford Designers & Illustrators Ltd
Printed in Great Britain by Athenæum Press Ltd, Gateshead, Tyne-and-Wear

Contents

Introduction   5

TERM 1

UNIT

1 Making words work   Narrative   9

2 Making sentences work   Narrative   15

3 Using verbs   Narrative   21

4 Using connectives   Narrative   27

5 Complex sentences (1) – connectives   Journalistic writing   33

6 Complex sentences (2) – clauses   Non-chronological report   39

7 Punctuation   Non-chronological report   45

8 Test preparation (1) – writing stylish scenes   Narrative   51

9 Test preparation (2) – writing stylish scenes   Narrative   57

TERM 2

UNIT

10 Who dunnit?   Narrative   63

11 Formal language (1)   Advertisement   69

12 Complex sentences (3) – punctuation   Public notice   75

13 Complex sentences (4) – variation   Narrative   82

14 Contracting sentences   Narrative   88

15 Conditionals   Discussion   94

16 Revision (1) – narrative writing   Narrative   100

17 Revision (2) – formal writing   Discussion   106

TERM 3

UNIT

18 Test preparation (3) –
sentences and paragraphs   Narrative   113

19 Comparing text types (1) –
narrative/recount   Narrative   119

20 Comparing text types (2) –
report/explanation   Explanation   125

21 Comparing text types (3) –
instruction/explanation   Explanation   131

22 Formal language (2)   Public document   137

23 Complex sentences (5)   Recount   143

24 Developing a theme   Song lyric/poem   149

25 Developing a style   Discussion   155

Introduction

Grammar Success is about teaching children how to use grammar to improve their writing. It provides materials, not only to deepen children's grammatical understanding, but also to refine their grammatical skills and to enable them to apply these to their own writing.

Teaching grammatical skills

The course helps pupils to understand grammar but also to become skilful in these key grammatical areas:

- **Sentence construction** – the ability to construct, vary, and control a variety of sentence structures.
- **Punctuation** – the ability to use punctuation to indicate to the reader how a text should be read.
- **Language effects** – the ability to enhance writing, using words powerfully and effectively, plus handling such effects as *simile*, *metaphor*, and *alliteration*.
- **Cohesion** – the ability to create cohesive links within and between sentences, paragraphs, and texts.

It is worth remembering that when children settle down to write, the task can be quite daunting. A good writer has to handle skilfully such basics as handwriting, spelling, and punctuation, as well as controlling sentences and thinking about what to say. Indeed, many children struggle with writing because they fall at the first post: their minds are taken up by worrying over such basics as 'Where does the full stop go?'. If such basic skills are not reasonably automatic, if children are not confident at handling grammar, then their ability to compose will be held back.

This course is founded upon the proposition that becoming skilful at grammar actually can liberate children as writers. The more adept children are at using these skills in their writing, the more freedom they will have to focus upon the actual act of creative composition. Good writers are skilful at handling the building blocks of language. Ted Hughes knew where to put full stops; he was able to focus upon the act of creation.

Teaching sequences

Grammar Success is built around the National Literacy Framework sentence level objectives, and also supports the programmes of study in the Northern Ireland English Curriculum and those of English Language 5–14. However, where there are gaps in the framework, these have been addressed. Additions and slight alterations have been made in the light of teachers' experience of using the framework in the classroom.

In planning the course, attention has been paid to ensuring that sensible links have been created between sentence and text level objectives. After all, the purpose of the sentence level work is to improve the ability to read and write different texts.

Each unit in *Grammar Success* facilitates the teaching of specific sentence level grammar points through a sequence of three or four sessions. The 'one off' lesson too often fails as children need a chance to revisit and to apply what they have been learning. To address this, each unit leads pupils through these three/four stages of learning, using all elements of the course:

Session 1 Activities that introduce children to a particular sentence level feature through whole class use of an OHT and consolidation in a photocopy master (PCM A).

Session 2 Investigating the use of the feature through reading and focused language work in the pupils' book and follow-up PCM B activity.

Session 3 Applying the feature to improve their written work, through shared and independent writing, based on work in the pupils' book.

Session 4 Developing the feature through extension, revision or editing of the writing begun in Session 3.

While a full range of texts and outcomes are provided in the pupils' book, children will gain greater understanding of the grammar if they are taught the four sessions using all three elements of the course.

How the sessions work

Session 1 Session 1 uses an OHT to introduce the grammatical objective to the children. This part of the session should be lively and interactive. The majority of basic grammar teaching can be accomplished through active whole-class teaching. OHTs have a number of advantages over using a worksheet or working on a board:

- It is easy to check that children are watching and engaged.
- The text can be annotated in response to children's ideas. Different features can be underlined in different colours to draw attention to different aspects of a text.
- The text can be projected onto a whiteboard which can be written upon.

Once time has been spent as a whole class looking at an objective, the class moves into independent activities. These are designed around a PCM (all PCMs are flagged) that provides an activity devised to deepen children's understanding and confirm what they have been taught as a whole class. Many of the PCMs are differentiated to allow for pupils who may struggle or who need an extra challenge. Or they could be used flexibly as a homework resource.

By the end of Session 1, pupils should be in a position to define their understanding of the objective. Definition needs to relate not merely to discussing what the feature is – but should also cover how it is used. Pupils may like to keep a literacy glossary into which definitions and points about writing are written. Class wall charts are useful as a way of providing a reminder.

Session 2 uses the pupils' book, plus the PCMs in the Teacher's Guide.

The pupils' book activities focus upon the grammatical feature in the context of wide-ranging stimulus texts. Pupils are asked comprehension questions on each text before moving into activities that focus upon the grammatical feature in use. Session 2 thus moves children's understanding further on, because it is designed to look at the objective in context.

Movement through the session is quite simple – read the stimulus text and think about what it means. Then revisit the text and look carefully at how it has been written. In this way children are encouraged to read as writers – looking constantly at the structures and grammatical features that writers use to create texts and gain effects. The teacher's notes offer questions to ask and points to make in a whole-class introduction.

This time the independent activities are in the pupils' book. Activity A consists of comprehension questions that dig under the skin of the text, deepening children's understanding. Activity B focuses upon the use of the sentence level feature within the text. It revisits the grammatical feature introduced in Session 1 and considers its use within a text.

The plenary, outlined in the teacher's notes, draws all the children together to reconfirm what is known about the sentence level feature. This process should put the large majority of children in the class in a position to understand the feature and to recognize how writers use it effectively within texts. References outwards to other texts are, of course, useful.

By the end of Session 2, pupils have critically reflected upon the use of the objective through their reading.

Session 3 relates again to the text in the pupils' book, which now becomes a model for children's own writing. The teacher's notes describe in detail how to carry out shared writing, demonstrating how to use the grammatical feature in the process of drafting a new text as part of activity C.

The role of shared writing cannot be underestimated as a key approach to teaching writing. During shared writing a number of different teaching strategies can be brought into play:

1 *Demonstration* – the teacher shows children how to use the feature, talking through the writing, explaining its use as an 'expert writer'. The children's role is to sit and listen carefully. Obviously, the modelling needs to be swift and engaging or children may grow restless. However, if the teacher writes directly onto an OHT this has the advantage of the teacher being able to look at the class at a glance, aiding control and drawing children's attention to the teaching points. The teacher rehearses sentences aloud and constantly rereads, checking the writing.

2 *Whole class composition* – having demonstrated how to use an objective, the teacher moves onto involving the children in actively writing. Obviously this process has to be lively and engaging, challenging children to refine their contributions. There is a danger of merely accepting the first thought that comes into the children's heads. They should be asked to explain ideas and discuss why one idea might be more effective than another. Building in time for children briefly to discuss ideas in pairs is also useful as a way of involving every pupil.

3 *Supported writing* – using whiteboards or notebooks, children have an attempt at using the feature within one or two sentences. This can be supported by a list of ideas, a writing frame or by pair work. The teacher can then check that children can use the objective in a controlled situation, within a few sentences. Once they are confident, children can move into more extended independent composition.

A photocopiable Reminder Sheet in the Teacher's Guide (flagged R) provides a summary, defining the grammatical feature and giving guidance on how to use it effectively in writing. This could be adapted or added to by the children in the light of their thoughts. Rudimentary understandings can be refined over time. These sheets might be added to the children's literacy glossary, put onto an OHT as a whole class reminder, or enlarged and displayed as a poster.

Session 3 moves into pupils writing their own work, drawing on the shared writing experience. As pupils write independently the teacher may wish to work with a group that struggles or to stretch the top end.

Session 4 extends and develops understanding and allows pupils to work on a piece over time. The writing may be continued in later sessions; alternatively, the teacher may revise or edit a piece of previously written work. The Teacher's Guide specifies whether work to be revised/edited should be class writing from Session 3 or pupils' writing (copied onto OHT). The teacher models and supports this stage of the writing process. The emphasis in Session 4 moves to pupils' contributions (i.e. supported writing). Pupils then transfer this learning to the writing they began in Session 3. The focus of the plenary is generally on evaluating the revision, and the impact the learning has had on pupils' individual writing.

Children should become used to concentrating hard during writing. Just before they start it is helpful to remind them of the particular features they should include. As they move through the units, each feature should be added to their growing repertoire of grammatical skills.

End of year hurdles

One of the difficulties that many teachers face is knowing what children should have achieved by the end of any given year. The grid below provides a clear set of markers to aim for. The list relates directly to the level descriptors, the programmes of study, and the literacy framework.

Many children will achieve more than this – the grid provides a base line. A few will not reach this level. However, the grid lists key aspects that can be used as a focus for teaching, for marking, for monitoring, and for target setting.

Of course, not everything has to be tackled at once. During the course of Year 6, children should become more adept in demonstrating the features described. If children can demonstrate these features frequently in their everyday writing, they will be on target for achieving a confident level 5.

Assessing writing

Guidance on marking and assessing pupils' briefer written responses is built in to each unit in this *Teacher's Guide* through assessment notes and model answers. Page 8 offers an example of a child's response (and a teacher's assessment) to a longer written task in activity C of the pupils' book. The sample is by a Year 6 child who has been working on Unit 5 in the pupils' book.

Sentence construction	Punctuation	Language effects	Cohesion	Purpose and organization
Secure control of complex sentences, understanding how clauses can be manipulated to achieve different effects. Write sentences in an appropriate and effective style, in relation to text type, audience and purpose. Use conditional sentences and the passive voice.	Demarcate most sentences correctly using the Y5 range of punctuation marks. Secure the use of the comma to demarcate grammatical boundaries and to separate elements of a sentence, such as short phrases, clauses or items in a list. Begin to make use of other punctuation marks, such as the semi-colon. **End of Year 6: Statement of Objectives**	Use well-chosen phrases such as adverbials; adventurous and precise vocabulary; and other techniques, such as sentence variation or figurative language, to contribute to the effectiveness of writing.	Use pronouns and tenses accurately to establish textual cohesion and to avoid ambiguity. Use a range of connecting words and phrases appropriately in different text types. Use paragraphs to distinguish the structure of different texts. Relate events logically so that writing is coherent and provides good coverage of the main topic. Use the range of different types of connective to write coherently.	Plan quickly and effectively, including the conclusion. Polish own poetry for performance. Use IT to plan, revise and edit writing for publication. Discuss and select appropriate style and form to suit specific purpose and audience, drawing on knowledge of different texts. Write with appropriate pace. In narrative, create characters with some significant interaction between them, through direct or reported speech, building characterization through action, description and characters' responses. In non-fiction structures, write appropriately, including relevant introduction and clear presentation of information or points which lead to a well-drawn conclusion, often relating the subject to the reader.

Yesterday, in the Australian open, two British men challenged each other to a place in the fourth round. Tim Henman, the number 6 seed, beat Greg Rusedski 6-4, 6-3, 1-6, 6-3, in a nailbiting match in which, on the day, the better man won.

Greg said afterwards that, had he won against Tim, the tournament trophy could have been his. He was clearly unhappy on more than one occasion when he considered the line judge's call to be inaccurate.

Menman commented that he played 'a pretty smart game considering it was a difficult occasion for both of us.' Lucy Henman, his wife, is Tim's lucky charm. She cheered him to victory but will Tim be quite so lucky against Jonas Bjorkman in the next round?

TERM 1

UNIT 1

Making words work

The purpose of this unit is to revise key word classes and their use in writing. It also focuses on using a shift in narrator as a narrative technique.

NLS coverage

Key objective

SL 1 To revise the different word classes from Year 5

Learned through:

TL Writing composition
6 To manipulate narrative perspective by writing in the voice and style of a text; writing a story with two different narrators

Assessment criteria

SL By the end of this unit, pupils should be able to identify, use and discuss the impact of nouns, adjectives, verbs, adverbs and prepositions within their own, and other people's, writing.

TL Writing composition
Children should be able to write a narrative using two narrators.

Session 1

You will need OHT 1 and PCM 1A.

Shared reading

1 Display OHT 1, read through the text and take first impressions.

2 Take suggestions for what different words might mean.

Sentence level work

1 As a class, go through each word and decide what word class it probably belongs to.

2 Make a list, looking for three of each of the following: nouns, adjectives, verbs, adverbs, prepositions.

3 Some of the words have clues in the spelling. What are these?

Independent activities

Direct pupils to PCM 1A. This is a series of weak sentences in which some of the words used could be improved. The words to improve are underlined. The task is to write down the word class, and make the sentences more effective by using stronger vocabulary.

Plenary

Summarize definitions of word classes. Listen to suggestions for improvements to the sentences.

Session 2

You will need pupils' book 4, Unit 1, pages 10–11, and PCM 1B.

Shared reading

1 What time of year is it?

2 What sort of story does this come from?

3 Give two clues to back up your answer.

4 What might have happened between Polly and Gwendal just before this scene?

5 Support your idea.

Sentence level work

1 Identify a noun, an adjective, a verb and a preposition.

2 How does this sentence begin to build up tension? *Polly didn't hear the garden gate swing open, didn't hear the soft footfalls on the grass.*

3 Add an adverb to this sentence. Try it out in different places. *I dumped my bag in the hall and called up the stairs.*

4 Drop a clause into this sentence: *Polly screamed.* For example: *Polly, <u>dashing for the door</u>, screamed.*

Independent activities

Children complete questions A and B in the pupils' book. Use PCM 1B to revise word classes and practise improving a piece of writing.

Plenary

Use the plenary to focus on the answers to question B. Listen to suggestions for improving the writing on the PCM. Emphasize that when writing the children should always pause, think if there are other words that could be used, and select the most powerful and appropriate.

Session 3

You will need pupils' book 4, Unit 1, pages 10–11, and the Reminder Sheet.

Shared writing

Explain the task in question 11. Put the suggested storyline into four boxes so that everyone can see the basic structure. Return to the original and see how these parts have been written. Draw attention to the way in which the shift in narrator has been achieved.

Write together
Demonstrate how to start writing your own version, and then take ideas from the class. Reread each section in the original and use them to trigger ideas. For instance, start with description, triggered by the weather, e.g.

The sun blazed. Heat shimmered on the tarmac road, making the end of the lane seem to shiver. Sam looked back over her shoulder. In the doorway she could just make out the dark figure. It was Balti. She couldn't see his face but she knew that he would be watching her every move, making sure that she made her way down the lane towards the shops.

Balti suddenly came alive. He raised his hands and waved frantically. She could see his mouth open in a scream. Then it hit her, 'Watch out!' he was screaming.

A dark shadow rushed towards her...

Independent writing activity

The class write their own version, following the instructions in the pupils' book.

Plenary

Listen to some examples. Highlight any good use of vocabulary.

Session 4

You will need a section of work you have written, or one written by a pupil, on OHT, and the Reminder Sheet.

Shared writing

Remind pupils of the focus – writing an exciting scene, carefully choosing words and making a shift in narrator.

Write together
Use examples to highlight good use of vocabulary, a successful shift in narrator. Work with the class on a few weaker examples.

Independent writing activity

Everyone revises to secure:
- effective vocabulary
- a successful shift in narrator
- a clause dropped into at least one sentence
- varying sentences for dramatic impact.

Plenary

Listen and comment on improvements, comparing the original with the new version.

Assessment

Pupils should be able to:
- identify, use and discuss the impact of nouns, adjectives, verbs, adverbs and prepositions within their own, and other people's, writing
- write an exciting narrative scene using two narrators.

Model answers

Pupils' book 4 A

1 They could be brother and sister, or cousins, or just friends.
2 A cat or some other smallish creature.
3 Somebody or something attacks Polly.
4 The narrator tells the first part – then a character.
5 *A grey shape streaked; misty-looking; swept; dead; whispering.*

Pupils' book 4 B

6 Answers will vary – ensure verbs are 'powerful'!
7 Example: *The wind shook leaves off the trees. Wind chimes began to peal.*
8 Answers will vary, e.g. *Polly turned cautiously…*
9 Examples: *the line of the <u>tall</u> tree; I <u>reached</u> home; he <u>was staring</u> at her; and <u>shouted</u> up the stairs.*
10 Example: *Polly, <u>seized by fear</u>, turned.*

1A   Making words work

adjective; adjective; verb; verb; adverb; adverb; noun (×4). Check sentences are strengthened by the selection of more powerful and precise verbs, nouns, etc.

1B   Making words work

noun; adjective; verb; adverb. Example: *She picked a <u>sunflower</u>*, etc. Check that vocabulary has been strengthened.

The underlined words in the following sentences are weak. Write down their word class, then make the sentences more effective by using stronger vocabulary.

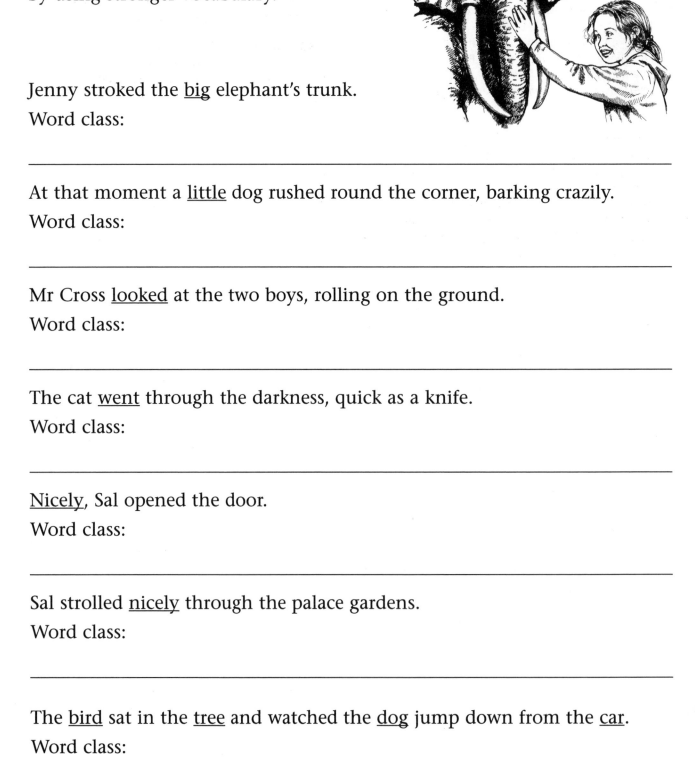

Jenny stroked the <u>big</u> elephant's trunk.
Word class:

_____

At that moment a <u>little</u> dog rushed round the corner, barking crazily.
Word class:

_____

Mr Cross <u>looked</u> at the two boys, rolling on the ground.
Word class:

_____

The cat <u>went</u> through the darkness, quick as a knife.
Word class:

_____

<u>Nicely</u>, Sal opened the door.
Word class:

_____

Sal strolled <u>nicely</u> through the palace gardens.
Word class:

_____

The <u>bird</u> sat in the <u>tree</u> and watched the <u>dog</u> jump down from the <u>car</u>.
Word class:

_____

Write down the word classes of the underlined words, then improve the sentences by using stronger vocabulary.

She picked a <u>flower</u>.
Word class:

_____

The <u>hot</u> sun sizzled.
Word class:

_____

The old gentleman <u>got</u> out of the car with some difficulty.
Word class:

_____

Sal ate the cream doughnut <u>nicely</u>.
Word class:

_____

Improve this paragraph by strengthening the vocabulary. You can add or change words.

Poppy walked down the street. She stopped by a car and decided to cross over. At the other side she saw something in the gutter. It was a ring. She got it. It was a nice ring. She put it on. 'That's mine,' a voice said. Poppy went quickly up the street. She could hear someone behind her.

_____

_____

_____

_____

_____

_____

1 Making words work

Nouns are words that name somebody or something, e.g. *The cat smiled.*

When you write, use precise nouns, e.g.

The Siamese sat in the Rolls Royce rather than *The cat sat in the car.*

Adjectives are words that describe somebody or something, e.g. *The red cat smiled.* They usually come before a noun, but can come after verbs such as *be, get, seem, look,* e.g. *The cat seems hot.*

When you write, use adjectives with care. Do not use too many. Do not use obvious ones. You do not always need one. Try using something a little unusual – that tells the reader something new, e.g. *The skinny elephant sat down* rather than *The large/huge/big elephant sat down.*

Verbs are words that express an action, happening, process or state, e.g. *The cat sat on the mat.* They can be thought of as 'doing' or 'being' words, e.g. *The cat is on the mat.*

When you write, choose verbs with care. Try to use powerful and expressive verbs that really explain what is happening, e.g. *The man hobbled down the road* rather than *The man went down the road.*

Adverbs are words that give extra meaning to a verb, e.g. *The cat sat carefully on the mat.*

When you write, choose adverbs with care. Sometimes you do not need one, e.g. *She strolled* rather than *She walked slowly.*

Adverbs are like detectives. They tell the reader the following:
- how – *she ran slowly*
- where – *she ran outside*
- when – *she ran yesterday*
- how often – *she ran regularly*.

You can often move adverbs in a sentence to great effect, e.g.

Carefully, she opened the door rather than *She opened the door carefully.*

UNIT 2

Making sentences work

The purpose of this unit is to revise controlling and varying sentences for different effects. It is related to writing a scene in the same style as a popular author, varying sentences.

NLS coverage

Key objective

SL 1 To revise re-expressing sentences in a different order; the construction of complex sentences from Year 5

Learned through:

TL Writing composition
6 To manipulate narrative perspective by writing in the voice and style of a text

Assessment criteria

SL By the end of this unit, pupils should be able to identify, discuss, use, control and vary a range of sentence structures in their own, and in relation to other people's writing.

TL Writing composition
Children should be able to write a short scene in the style of an author.

Session 1

You will need OHT 2 and PCM 2A.

Shared reading

1 Display OHT 2, and discuss it with the class. What do you think they saw in *that awful room*? What do we know about the main character, his father and their relationship? Who exactly is the *baby sister*?

2 Why is this quite easy to read?

Sentence level work

1 What do you notice about the style of the writer? Comment on – words, sentences, paragraphs.

2 Find and list:
- a short sentence for dramatic impact
- a short 'non' sentence
- a question that makes the reader wonder
- a compound sentence joined by 'and' used to make the sentence flow
- a complex sentence using 'so' as a connective.

Independent activities

Direct pupils to PCM 2A in which they are asked to imitate a range of sentence structures. You might need to imitate the first example, e.g.
'No!'

Plenary

Go carefully through PCM 2A, building up a repertoire of sentence structures that can be called upon during writing. This will be a reminder of work carried out in previous years.

Session 2

You will need pupils' book 4, Unit 2, pages 12–13, and PCM 2B.

Shared reading

1 What effect on the reader is the writer trying to achieve?

2 How successful is the writer?

3 Which part is most dramatic?

4 Why doesn't Caveman speak?

5 What does *He raised and lowered one shoulder* suggest?

Sentence level work

1 Find examples of:
   ■ a dramatic sentence
   ■ a descriptive sentence
   ■ a short sentence
   ■ a long sentence.

2 In these complex sentences, which is the main clause? (underlined)
   Stanley had no idea why she was showing it to him.
   'It's only toxic when it's wet.'
   The Warden turned to face Mr. Sir, who was sitting on the fireplace hearth.

3 What connective comes at the start of each subordinate clause?

4 What is the function of the subordinate clause?

Independent activities

Children complete questions A and B in the pupils' book. Use PCM 2B to reinforce understanding of the different types of sentence.

Plenary

Use the plenary to run through the answers. Use the PCM to emphasize the checklist of possible sentence types. Remind children that in the next session you will be using these to write some narrative.

Session 3

You will need pupils' book 4, Unit 2, pages 12–13, and the Reminder Sheet.

Shared writing

Explain the task in question 9 – writing a passage in the same style, using a similar sequence of events, remembering to vary sentences for effect and to choose words carefully.

Write together

Put boxes round the suggested sequence so that the children can clearly see the different scenes/paragraphs needed. Use the boxed scenes and the original to help compose a similar piece of writing.

For example:
The Warden brought out a small wooden box with white, ivory handles. 'Look at this, Caveman.' She lifted the lid and he stared into the box.
'This is where I keep my little pet. Do you see the zigzag pattern? Look at the way it sways from side to side.'
The snake hissed. Stanley was not too sure what she was going to do with it. He rubbed the palms of his hands on his shorts.
The Warden picked the snake up, squeezing its neck just below the head so that it could not reach her....

Independent writing activity

The children write their own version in the same way. They need to think about what the container will be and what might be in it, e.g. a jar with a deadly scorpion.

Plenary

Listen to versions. Draw attention to well chosen vocabulary and controlled sentence variation used for dramatic effect.

Session 4

You will need a section of work you have written, or one written by a pupil, on OHT, and the Reminder Sheet.

Shared writing

Remind pupils of the focus – using effective vocabulary (from the previous unit), varying sentences for effect, and following the basic sequence of scenes as a planning device.

Write together

Use good examples to identify strengths in writing. Use weaker examples to show how these might be improved.

Independent writing activity

Pupils work on their own or in pairs to revise and improve. They must check for:
   ■ effective vocabulary
   ■ controlled and varied sentence structure for dramatic effect
   ■ accurate punctuation.

Plenary

Listen to improved versions set against the original – discuss whether changes have been improvements. Just before collecting in, ask children to check each other's writing for correct punctuation.

Model answers

Pupils' book 4 A

1 The word *Warden* suggests prison; the words *store* and *pinkie* are not commonly used in the UK; you get rattlesnakes in America and Australia.
2 Maybe he looks or behaves like one.
3 Someone has stolen Mr. Sir's sunflower seeds.
4 Answers will vary. She doesn't seem the sort who dresses up or goes out so there must be some other reason. Maybe she enjoys the danger of using venom in the polish, or maybe it makes her feel more powerful.
5 Mr. Sir might die; maybe there is a fight or Caveman runs away!
6 Perhaps he had wrongly accused Caveman; maybe she doesn't like Mr. Sir; maybe she just wanted to demonstrate her power.

Pupils' book 4 B

7 and 8 Answers will vary – pupils should give reasons.

2A   Making sentences work

Answers will vary. Check that sentence type is imitated.

2B   Making sentences work

Sentences	Sentence type
Quietly, they made their way towards the compound.	Adverb starter to increase tension
Solly, dressed in a white robe that was edged with red fur, strode in.	Complex sentence to add detail
Where did the tunnel lead?	Question
'Run for it!'	Exclamation
Solly picked up his coat and went out into the night.	Compound sentence
Whenever she stopped, the guards shouted at her.	Connective starter
Behind the house was a small shed.	Preposition starter
Solly smiled at his friend.	Simple sentence

2A *Making sentences work*

Imitate each of these sentence types.

1   Short exclamation for surprise: *'Help!'*

_____

2   Short, simple sentence for dramatic effect: *They ran.*

_____

3   Compound sentence for easy flow: *Solly turned the corner and made his way down the street.*

_____

4   Question to make the reader wonder: *Why was she showing him the snake?*

_____

5   Complex sentence to add in extra detail: *Solly, wearing a bright red tie, entered the room.*

_____

6   Complex sentence to add extra information: *Solly ran fast so that he would have time to hide.*

_____

7   Adverb starter to increase tension: *Slowly, she edged the door open.*

_____

8   'ing' or 'ed' starter to focus on action: *Screaming with agony, Tom fell.*

_____

9   Connective starter to emphasize a reason, etc: *Although they were weary, they marched on.*

_____

10 Preposition starter to emphasize 'where': *At the end of the lane stood an old house.*

_____

Use the table to match the sentences to the sentence types.

Sentence types

Exclamation
Simple sentence
Compound sentence
Question
Adverb starter to increase tension
Connective starter
Preposition starter
Complex sentence to add detail

Sentences	Sentence type
Quietly, they made their way towards the compound.	
Solly, dressed in a white robe that was edged with red fur, strode in.	
Where did the tunnel lead?	
'Run for it!'	
Solly picked up his coat and went out into the night.	
Whenever she stopped, the guards shouted at her.	
Behind the house was a small shed.	
Solly smiled at his friend.	

2 | *Making sentences work*

Good writers vary their sentences to create different effects. Here are some useful sentence types – remember to use them in your own writing.

1 Short exclamation for surprise:
'Help!'

2 Short, simple sentence for dramatic effect:
They ran.

3 Compound sentence for easy flow:
Solly turned the corner and made his way down the street.

4 Question to make the reader wonder:
Why was she showing him the snake?

5 Complex sentence to add in extra detail:
Solly, wearing a bright red tie, entered the room.

6 Complex sentence to add extra information:
Solly ran fast so that he would have time to hide.

7 Adverb starter to increase tension:
Slowly, she edged the door open.

8 'ing' or 'ed' starter to focus on action:
Screaming with agony, Tom fell.

9 Connective starter to emphasize a reason, etc:
Although they were weary, they marched on.

10 Preposition starter to emphasize 'where':
At the end of the lane stood an old house.

11 Sentence fragment for effect:
Not a word.

12 Descriptive sentence:
The box was dark brown, edged with thin gold stripes.

13 Action sentence:
He threw himself forwards, diving between the two guards.

Remember: Always check your punctuation.

Using verbs

The purpose of this unit is to consolidate basic understanding of how to use powerful verbs effectively plus a revision of the nature of active and passive verbs. It links with work in Year 5 and work coming in term 2.

NLS coverage

Key objectives

| SL | 2 To revise earlier work on verbs and to understand the terms *active* and *passive*; to be able to transform a sentence from active to passive, and vice versa

| SL | 3 To note and discuss how changes from active to passive affect the word order and sense of a sentence

Learned through:

| TL | Writing composition
6 To manipulate narrative perspective by writing in the voice and style of a text

Assessment criteria

| SL | By the end of this unit, pupils should be able to identify a verb, discuss its impact and select powerful verbs when writing; identify active and passive and transform from one to the other.

| TL | Writing composition
Children should be able to write a short scene in the style of an author, using verbs effectively, selecting words and sentences with control and care.

Session 1

You will need OHT 3 and PCM 3A.

Shared reading

1 Display OHT 3, covering up all the sentences except the first one. Which is the verb? What is its job in the sentence? Can you think of a more powerful one?

2 Look at sentence 2. Is this better? How can the sentence be made more dramatic? Demonstrate how to tighten *was slithering* to *slithered*.

3 Look at sentence 3. Is this a powerful verb? What does it tell us about Mr Throg? Make the point that a well chosen word really helps you write effectively, especially creating action and character.

Sentence level work

1 Look at sentences 4 and 5. What is the difference? The first is active – so the subject (*the teacher*) performs the action. As the second is in the passive, the subject (*the cream doughnut*) is on the receiving end of the verb, and who performed the action is uknown.

2 The rest of the sentences are all in the passive. Play a quick game of 'Who dunnit?' by hiding the end of the sentences. Can they guess who or what scratched the car, etc.?

3 Then transform each one into active. For example: *The car was scratched by the goat* becomes *The goat scratched the car.*

Independent activities

Direct pupils to PCM 3A, which is in three sections. Pupils are asked to improve the verbs; transform the sentences from passive back into active; then try the other way round.

Plenary

Run through the children's work on PCM 3A. Summarize with them what they know about verbs and consolidate active/passive.

Session 2

You will need pupils' book 4, Unit 3, pages 14–15, and PCM 3B.

Shared reading

1 Read the passage on page 14 and then the poem.

2 Why is the *he* following the girl?

3 How old do you think he might be – are there clues?

4 What sort of story might this be from? Support your views.

5 Explain the 'twist' in the poem.

Sentence level work

1 Change the underlined verbs to alter the mood of the opening. For example:

Then he <u>noticed</u> her, just a few feet from him, <u>wandering</u> through the bracken towards the lighthouse.

2 Discuss how this changes the effect and meaning.

3 In the poem, rewrite this sentence in the active:
A glass in the kitchen was smashed.
To do this you will have to decide who did it! (E.g. *I smashed a glass in the kitchen.*)

Independent activities

Children complete questions A and B in the pupils' book. Use PCM 3B for practice in changing verbs to alter the tone of some sentences and for further work on transforming sentences from passive to active.

Plenary

Use the plenary to go over the work so far.

Session 3

You will need pupils' book 4, Unit 3, pages 14–15, and the Reminder Sheet.

Shared writing

Explain that the task in question 9 is to use the same sort of structure to write a short scene in the manner of the writer. Box up each scene to make the sequence clear. Remind pupils to use powerful verbs and to avoid the passive.

Write together

Demonstrate a line or two and then involve the class. For example:

Then she noticed him, across the park, staring at the ducks. 'Hang on, I'm coming,' she yelled. Solly's head jerked up. He scanned the park and saw her running towards him. Without thinking, he ran. She pounded after him but by the time she reached the pond he had disappeared...

Independent writing activity

Before writing, the children need to decide on the two characters and where they are. Then they use the same basic structure and write – bearing in mind the need to select verbs with care.

Plenary

Listen to examples and comment on well chosen verbs that add pace and power to the scene.

Session 4

You will need a section of work you have written, or one written by a pupil, on OHT, and the Reminder Sheet.

Shared writing

Remind pupils of the focus – writing interesting scenes, carefully choosing powerful verbs, avoiding the passive, and thinking about the order of the words in sentences.

Write together

Work on good examples, identifying how the verb works. Work on several weaker examples, changing verbs to strengthen the impact.

Independent writing activity

Children revise and read their writing aloud in pairs, to listen to the impact. They prepare for a class reading.

Plenary

End with a class reading – as many children as possible reading their writing aloud.

Assessment

Sentence level
Pupils should be able to identify a verb, discuss its impact and select powerful verbs when writing; identify active and passive and transform from one to the other.

Writing composition
Children should be able to write a short scene in the style of an author, using verbs effectively, selecting words and sentences with control and care

Model answers

Pupils' book 4 ⬜ **A**

1 Afraid; it says she was *out of her mind with terror.* Other vocabulary used to describe her backs this up.
2 He is desperate to get to her – he runs and shouts after her; he shrieks *'No!'* when she disappears, unable to believe that she is gone; he keeps on running after her.
3 Suspense, tension, fear.
4 The speaker (child)!
5 Ensure pupils justify responses by referring to the texts.

Pupils' book 4 ⬜ **B**

6 *Scrambling, shouted, stumbled, clutching, thrusting, screaming, broke, raced, flailing, yawned, shrieked, pelted, fell, opened*
7 To create and maintain the drama.
8 *I scratched the car. I ruined the carpet. The cat swallowed the goldfish.*

⬜ **3A**   Using verbs ▯

1 Answers will vary, e.g. *The corgis <u>rushed</u> across the bedroom towards the door; Solly <u>grabbed</u> the knife from Berger's mighty paw; Sullivan <u>stared</u> at the diamond, knowing it was worth a million.*
2 *The robber crashed the new Mercedes. The police questioned the robber. The dog led the police astray.*
3 *The police van was stolen. They were shown a quick route. The bead was swallowed.*

⬜ **3B**   Using verbs ▯

1 Answers will vary, e.g. *She <u>crawled</u> onto the tree's lowest branch.*
2 *The cat broke the glass bowl. The naughty boy typed the letter. The rat chased the cat. The toddler kicked Solly.*

1 Rewrite these sentences using more powerful verbs.

■ The corgis <u>moved</u> across the bedroom towards the door.

_____

■ Solly <u>took</u> the knife from Berger's mighty paw.

_____

■ Sullivan <u>looked</u> at the diamond, knowing it was worth a million.

_____

2 Change these sentences from passive into active.

■ The new Mercedes was crashed by a robber.

_____

■ The robber was questioned by the police.

_____

■ The police were led astray by the dog.

_____

3 Change these sentences from active into passive.

■ The robbers stole the police van.

_____

■ A traffic warden showed them a quick route.

_____

■ The baby swallowed the bead.

_____

3B Using verbs

1 Change the underlined verbs to alter the sense of these sentences.

a) She <u>leaped</u> onto the tree's lowest branch.

_____

b) The camera-man <u>touched</u> the camera just as it fell.

_____

c) The zebra <u>trotted</u> down the aisle.

_____

d) The police officer <u>glanced</u> at the suspicious-looking man.

_____

e) She <u>whispered</u> into her 2-way radio.

_____

f) The camel <u>scoffed</u> the rubber duck with evident joy.

_____

2 Change these sentences from passive to active.

a) The glass bowl was broken by the cat.

_____

b) The letter was typed by the naughty boy.

_____

c) The cat was chased by the rat.

_____

d) Solly was kicked by the toddler.

_____

3 | *Using verbs*

Choosing verbs

Verbs are words that express an action, happening, process or state. For example:

The cat <u>sat</u> on the mat.

They can be thought of as 'doing' or 'being' words. For example:

The cat <u>is</u> on the mat.

When you write, choose verbs with care. Try to use powerful and expressive verbs that really explain what is happening. For example:

The man <u>hobbled</u> down the road.

rather than

The man <u>went</u> down the road.

Verb chains

Sometimes two or more words make up a verb phrase, such as
I <u>have been waiting</u> for the last train to arrive.

Verb tenses

Verbs can be in the past (*I ran*) or present (*I run*). To make the future, you need to form a verb chain, for example:

Miss Sadie and I <u>will fly</u> home soon.

Active and passive

The active voice is clear and powerful. For example:

The dog bit the man.

It is quite clear who did what.

However, you can hide who performed the action by using the passive and turning the sentence around. For example:

The man was bitten.

The passive is good if you want to hide who did something or if it doesn't matter who did it (*Sand and cement were mixed together*).

If you want to identify the 'doer' of the action, you can use the word 'by'. For example:

The man was bitten by the dog.

UNIT 4

Using connectives

The purpose of this unit is to allow pupils to explore more fully the way in which writers use connecting words and phrases in different types of text. The focus here will be specifically upon first and third person accounts.

NLS coverage

Key objective

[SL] 4 To investigate connecting words and phrases:
- collect examples
- study how points are connected in different kinds of text
- classify useful examples for different kinds of text

Learned through:

[TL] **Reading comprehension and writing composition**
11, 14 To distinguish between biography and autobiography; to develop the skills of biographical and autobiographical writing in role

Assessment criteria

[SL] By the end of this unit, pupils should be able to find alternative connecting words and phrases; classify different types of connectives; select the most appropriate connectives for a particular piece of writing.

[TL] **Writing composition**
Children should be able to write in the first and third person in role.

Session 1

You will need OHT 4 and PCM 4A.

Shared reading

1 Ask pupils how they think they will feel on their last afternoon in primary school. Allow pupils two or three minutes to confer with a friend, and then take suggestions. Discuss the mix of emotions pupils have offered.

2 Explain that the text is about someone's final afternoon in school. Display and read OHT 4.

3 Discuss Anna's feelings. For each paragraph, discuss the principal emotions she experienced. Mark these on the OHT. Make sure that pupils explain how they know – referring to the text for evidence, as well as drawing upon their own experiences.

4 Discuss the characters in the text. What do pupils feel about Nicky and Anna? Again, encourage them to support their answers by reference to the text.

5 Look at other ways in which the writer has told us about the character of Miss McGoldrick. Focus on *gorgon gaze; thankfully; I breathed a sigh of relief...*

6 Consider the writer's use of the first person. How does this affect the piece? Does it add impact? In what way?

7 Draw pupils' attention to the structure of the text, which has separate sections:
- one paragraph of background
- the incident, and its development
- a link to later events.

Sentence level work

1 Explain that you will be looking at different types of connective: those used to link ideas within the text, and those which link ideas and information in the text to life at Elmbank School.

2 Ask pupils to find one example where the writer has linked the text to life at the school:
We lined up in the yard after dinner, as usual.

3 Can pupils identify the connective phrase in this sentence? It is *as usual*. Without being explicit, the writer has told us that this is something that happened every day. All of the devices the writer uses to tell us about the teacher tell us about day-to-day life at the school.

4 Move on to look at connectives within the text; encourage pupils to underline them.

5 Investigate how the writer has used punctuation to link ideas in the following sentences:

She swept the line with her gorgon gaze; silence fell, eyes were downcast, and children shuffled nervously.

It was the day we'd all been waiting for – our last session at Elmbank School.

I shouted with shock and pain – there was blood trickling down my leg.

6 With pupils, experiment with substituting connectives and punctuation. In some cases, pupils may want to practise separating longer sentences out into two shorter sentences and comparing effects.

7 Practise writing sentences using these structures to describe events in school recently.

Independent activities

1 Pupils complete PCM 4A. This asks them to use links from the OHT text to write a story of their own about a final session in school. The text leads them to write in the first person.

2 Work with a group of able writers to challenge their composition of complex sentences.

Plenary

Reread the text, and discuss the types of connective used. How many relate to time and sequence? Discuss why these are important in narrative.

Session 2

You will need pupils' book 4, Unit 4, pages 16–17, and PCM 4B.

Shared reading

1 Tell pupils that you are going to be reading another extract which relates to an incident in school. The story is set in America many years ago. They may find some evidence of this in the text.

2 Ask pupils to turn to page 16 in the pupils' book. Read aloud the extract from *Tom Sawyer* and ask for initial reactions. How would they have behaved in Tom's situation? What does Tom's behaviour tell us about how he felt about the girl? Ask them to infer what they can about the previous relationship between the two characters.

3 Discuss the way in which the children's relationship changes during the course of this extract. How long do pupils think the events take?

4 Is there anything unusual about the language? Draw pupils' attention to the way in which Mark Twain refers to Tom as 'the boy'. Why does he do this?

5 Consider the structure of the piece. Remind pupils of the structure of the OHT text. Does this text have the same structure? Identify the sections.

Sentence level work

1 Remind pupils that this unit of work focuses on connectives. Work with pupils to identify the connectives used in the text. Begin by focusing on connecting words and phrases. Ask pupils whether they have ever used these phrases. They may have used some, but others may be less obvious to them, e.g. *by and by, presently.* Ensure that pupils understand these connectives; discuss possible alternatives.

2 Look at how some of these connectives are placed at the beginning of sentences, while others occur in the middle. Experiment with altering sentences by moving clauses and connectives.

3 Look at other connective devices the writer has used, e.g. the way he refers to the main character and the girl (never by name, in this extract), and repetition of words such as *whispered.*

Independent activities

Children complete questions A and B in the pupils' book. Offer PCM 4B as an alternative activity in which pupils focus on connecting devices from the text.

Plenary

Reread the extract. Ask pupils what they think might happen next in the story, between these two characters.

Session 3

You will need pupils' book 4, Unit 4, pages 16–17, and the Reminder Sheet.

Shared writing

1 Explain to pupils that you will be writing about an incident in your own school experience.

2 Remind pupils that they have been collecting connectives from their reading. Build up a list of these connectives. Explain that you will select from them to add variety.

Write together

1 Begin by planning the piece. Remind pupils that you will need separate sections: one paragraph of

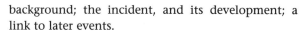

background; the incident, and its development; a link to later events.

2 Refer back to the two model texts from the OHT and pupils' book, so that pupils can see these sections again.

3 Tell the incident orally. Can pupils help to decide what could be in each section? Plot ideas onto a planning sheet.

4 Model the writing of the opening paragraph, selecting from the list of connectives.

Independent writing activity

Direct pupils to question 8 on page 17 of the pupils' book. They should work on their own plans and initial paragraphs.

Plenary

Invite pupils to share their opening paragraphs. Ask them to identify and explain their choice of narrative perspective (i.e. first/third person).

Session 4

You will need pupils' book 4, Unit 4, pages 16–17, and the Reminder Sheet.

Shared writing

Explain to pupils that you will now be working on the rest of the story. Remind them of the purpose of connectives – that they help readers see links between events and ideas in texts.

Write together

1 Return to the opening paragraph written in the previous session. Can it be improved? Refer pupils back to the list of connectives as you write, and encourage them to refer to a thesaurus for alternatives. Remind pupils that these are available electronically in many word processing packages.

2 Continue to model writing, drawing from the list of connectives.

Independent writing activity

Pupils complete their own writing.

Plenary

Discuss any new connectives pupils have used. Focus particularly on the position of connectives in sentences. Invite pupils to show how they have varied this.

Assessment

Comment upon pupils':
- ability to identify and classify connective words and phrases chosen by writers
- understanding of the range of connective devices, including use of punctuation and repetition, and their ability to use them in their writing
- ability to position connectives within sentences
- ability to manipulate sentences and replicate sentence structures
- ability to structure their biographical/ autobiographical accounts.

Model answers

Pupils' book 4 A

1 Tom seems to have been sent to sit next to her – perhaps for misbehaving? Pupils may give other explanations.

2 Tom seems to like the girl. He gives her a peach, and tries to engage her attention by drawing.

3 By drawing.

4 Calling Tom *the boy* emphasizes that he is talking to a girl; it may also be how the girl sees him.

5 Answers will vary.

Pupils' book 4 B

6 *and; but; by and by; once more; presently; when; then; now; for a time; at last; when it was finished*

7 The word *whispered* is always associated with the girl. It tells us about the classroom, and how all conversation has to be low level; it almost makes the reader whisper when reading.

4A Using connectives

Comment on the way in which pupils have used connectives, as well as whether they have managed to use all those on the OHT. Note whether pupils have been able to use punctuation to link ideas.

4B Using connectives

Pupils should have been able to replicate sentence structure.

Write a story about the last day before the Christmas holidays. Use the connectives from the OHT text. Remember that you can use punctuation to link ideas as well.

It was the day we'd all been waiting for _____ .

I had been _____ and

I was looking forward to _____ .

We _____ after _____ ,

as usual. There was _____

_____ , but I could see that

_____ . She _____ ;

_____ . Ahead of me,

_____ . _____ . Then

_____ .

_____ . Again, _____

I _____ , and _____ .

The _____ and we began to _____

for the last time. Daydreaming about _____ ,

I was just about to _____

when _____ .

Use some of these sentence structures and links from *Tom Sawyer* to write sentences of your own. Connectives to be reused have been underlined for you.

He sat down upon the end of the pine bench <u>and</u> the girl hitched herself away from him with a toss of her head.

_____

_____

<u>By and by</u> attention ceased from him, and the accustomed school murmur rose upon the dull air <u>once more</u>.

_____

_____

<u>Presently</u> the boy began to steal furtive glances at the girl.

_____

_____

<u>Now</u> the boy began to draw something on the slate, hiding his work with his left hand.

_____

_____

<u>For a time</u> the girl refused to notice, <u>but</u> her human curiosity presently began to manifest itself by hardly perceptible signs.

_____

_____

The boy worked on, <u>apparently</u> unconscious.

_____

_____

4 ⟩ *Using connectives*

Writers use connectives in many different ways. Sometimes, they are placed in the middle of sentences:

> *He sat down upon the end of the pine bench <u>and</u> the girl hitched herself away from him with a toss of her head.*
>
> *She thrust it away, <u>but</u> with less animosity.*

Sometimes, writers place connectives at the beginning of sentences:

> <u>*Presently*</u> *the boy began to steal furtive glances at the girl.*

Writers sometimes use connectives that link sentences, and connectives that link clauses within the sentence.

> <u>*By and by*</u> *attention ceased from him, <u>and</u> the accustomed school murmur rose upon the dull air <u>once more</u>.*

In stories, most of the connectives are about time – when things happen, and the order in which they happen.

Complex sentences (1) – connectives

The purpose of this unit is to reinforce and develop pupils' facility with sentence manipulation.

NLS coverage

Key objective

SL 5 To form complex sentences through using different connecting devices, evaluating which links work best

Learned through:

TL Writing composition
15, 16, 18 To develop a journalistic style; to use the styles and conventions of journalism to report on real or imagined events; to use IT to plan, revise and edit writing

Assessment criteria

SL By the end of this unit, pupils should be able to:
- identify simple and complex sentences
- combine ideas into sentences in different ways
- identify which is the most effective combination in any particular context.

TL Writing composition
Children should be able to write in a journalistic style.

Session 1

You will need OHT 5 and PCM 5A.

Shared reading

1 Explain to pupils that they will be looking at complex sentences and how writers use them to link ideas in journalism. Do any pupils have newspapers at home? Which ones? Do they read them?

2 Display, read and discuss the paragraphs on OHT 5. Do pupils feel they are journalistic? Look through the sentences for features that support their view. Refer to the use of language to create visual detail, rouse emotions and communicate action.

Sentence level work

1 Recap what pupils have already learned about connectives. In this unit, they will be looking at the way writers use them to build up sentences.

2 Look at the first sentence of the first paragraph.
Centre court was packed today for the women's singles final.
How much information is included in this sentence?

We have found out that:
- there was a capacity crowd
- the women's singles final was today
- people had come to see the women's singles final.

3 In the second sentence we discover that it was hot and tense. (We assume that the rise in temperature is due to excitement about the match. It was hot because of the sun.) How can we work this out? (Because the writer has linked the ideas for us.)

4 Consider the following:
- It was a hot day.
- There was a large crowd at Centre court.
- Everyone was very excited.
- The women's singles final was due to begin.
Experiment with different ways of combining this information into one or two sentences. Discuss which combinations are the most effective. It may be appropriate to discuss contexts of sentences – some may work better in one context than in another.

5 Repeat the procedure in 2–4 above with the other sentences on OHT 5.

Independent activities

Pupils complete PCM 5A, developing the bare outline of a sporting incident into continuous prose.

Plenary

Ask pupils to share what they have written with a partner. Each pair then selects one particularly rich sentence to share with another pair. Take brief feedback from each group of four.

Session 2

You will need pupils' book 4, Unit 5, pages 18–19, and PCM 5B.

Shared reading

1 This describes a sporting event with which pupils will not be familiar: chariot racing. Talk about the atmosphere at big sporting occasions – would the historic time make any difference?

2 Read page 18 of the pupils' book aloud. Allow time for pupils to reread the text to themselves before discussing the incidents. Why do they think the riot started? What would they have expected Gaius to do in the situation? How would they have felt there?

3 What writing genre is this? Pupils should recognize it as journalistic. Identify features and language which make it clear it is journalistic writing.

4 Identify humorous words and phrases (e.g. ... *security staff attacked rioters with heavy wooden sticks, and cutting personal remarks*). Discuss their impact.

Sentence level work

1 Explain to pupils that they will be looking at ways the author has linked clauses and sentences. Ask pupils to identify sentences with one, two and three clauses. Ask them to identify separate clauses, and then investigate how clauses are connected.
   - One clause: *This sport is quite dangerous enough already.*
   - Two clauses: *Interviewed after the incident, Gaius's manager admitted he was angry with his rider.* Pupils should note that the subordinate clause is placed before the main clause, separated by a comma. It is an adverbial clause – it describes <u>when</u> the manager said these things. The writer has used a temporal link (*after*). There are some words the author could have added, e.g. *When he was...* Why has he not done this? Would it have added anything?
   - Three clauses: *My fans are the most loyal in the world, and if my manager has me whipped he'll have all the windows in his town house broken in the*

middle of the night... Note how the writer has used *if... [then]* to link the second and third clauses, with a simple *and* for the first link.

2 Use these examples to model new sentences that might be included in a modern sports report. For example:
   - *The pitch was waterlogged enough already.*
   - *Speaking after the game, Houllier agreed that he was delighted with his team's performance.*
   - *My team are at the bottom of the league, but if the board gives players a bonus they might find players' confidence grows.*

3 Allow pupils to work in pairs to compose sentences of their own (not necessarily on a sporting theme). Check that all have a secure understanding. Collect some good examples to share.

Independent activities

Children complete questions A and B in the pupils' book. For pupils who have difficulty with clauses, offer PCM 5B as an alternative to B. This asks them to use sentence models without focusing on clauses.

Plenary

Discuss which sentences pupils chose, and which presented the most challenge. Did the longer sentences prove more difficult?

Session 3

You will need pupils' book 4, Unit 5, pages 18–19, and the Reminder Sheet.

Shared writing

1 Explain that you will be writing a piece about a sporting event. The shared piece will be about a fictional event; pupils will be writing about an event of their own choice – fictional or otherwise.

2 Begin by outlining your choice of a fictional event. Select one that will appeal equally to boys and girls, athletes and non-enthusiasts.

3 Map out the event's chronology (see PCM 5A as an example). Remind pupils that journalistic pieces have to contain a lot of information in a short space, which is why style is so important. They also have to attract readers' attention.

Write together

Begin the opening paragraph. Focus on the use of journalistic style, modelling the use of complex sentences to convey a number of ideas. Refer back to OHT 5 / the pupils' book text for ideas and models for sentences. Pupils may also offer suggestions from their own reading of newspapers, or TV journalism.

Independent writing activity

Pupils plan their own journalistic article. They should outline the piece and start the opening paragraph.

Work with pupils who may need support with planning, or challenge with the opening paragraph. An able group should manage a convincing opening.

Plenary

Pupils work with a response partner to develop and improve their opening. Ask them to feedback to the class on whether they enjoyed this activity, and what they found particularly challenging about it.

Suggest that pupils look at any newspapers they get at home for sports reports. It would be useful if they brought some in for the next session – owner's permission to be sought before the paper is cut up!

Session 4

You will need newspaper sports reports, pupils' book 4, Unit 5, pages 18–19, and the Reminder Sheet.

Shared writing

1 Pair pupils so that each has access to an article about a sporting event. Ask each pair to find one linking phrase that they particularly like. They should write this down for use later.

2 Reread the plan and opening paragraph for the article. Discuss whether it is 'good' journalism.

Write together

1 Carry on writing up the event. Invite pupils to contribute ideas and phrases from their reading. Comment specifically on the way in which connectives work to make sentences more effective. Experiment with different combinations and sequences. Remind pupils that this is a draft; there will be opportunities for revision at a later stage.

2 Model a strong final paragraph. This should summarize the event and may contain an emotional response. Draw attention to sentence structure.

Independent writing activity

Pupils continue with their own piece of writing. Support pupils who need help with their final paragraph.

Plenary

Return to the article you have written with the class. Discuss any revisions and the level of pictorial support. Pupils may wish to revise/complete their articles for homework, or in other English time.

Assessment

Pupils should be able to:
• identify clauses in sentences
• identify ways in which writers use links
• write in a journalistic style.
In responding to pupils' writing, comment on their use of a variety of sentence structures; offer support on linking clauses within sentences.

Model answers

Pupils' book 4 A
1 Answers will vary.
2 Answers will vary. Pupils will probably refer to rivalry, pride, etc.
3 Answers will vary. Pupils may feel that, although provoked, Gaius was still wrong to attack Scabius.
4 The horses were difficult to control, chariots moved at great speed, and drivers could easily be thrown off the chariot and trampled.
5 Answers will vary.

Pupils' book 4 B
6 Pupils should identify sentences with two or more clauses.
7 The sentences pupils create should follow the model of those from the text.

5A and 5B Complex sentences (1) – connectives
Answers will vary.

This report from a newspaper is not very interesting. The editor has sent it back to be improved. Can you help? Try to add detail and connect sentences.

Last weekend something happened at a football match.

_____

One of the players hit another player in the same team.

_____

He was sent off.

_____

He said the other player did something wrong.

_____

The manager was cross.

_____

The player might be suspended.

_____

The other player is not hurt.

_____

He said that football is a contact sport.

_____

This was one of three sendings off last weekend.

_____

Complex sentences (1) – connectives

Select sentences of different lengths from the pupils' book text. For each one, try to write two more sentences with the same structure.

	Example from text	My sentence 1	My sentence 2
Short sentence			
Average length sentence			
Longest sentence			

Writing for newspapers and magazines

Journalists write to inform and entertain. They have to make sure that people want to read what they have written – their jobs depend on it.

If you want to write like a journalist, you should remember to:

- write a good headline that will attract readers' attention
- really concentrate on the first paragraph – make readers want to read on
- be careful in selecting information – you won't have much space
- use photographs and captions to help readers understand the text, give extra information and break up the text
- make your last paragraph count – readers will remember the article better.

Connectives

Writers use connectives to build up sentences that can include a lot of information. Look at the sentence:

Centre court was packed today for the women's singles final.

This tells us that:

- there was a capacity crowd
- the women's singles final was today
- people had come to see the women's singles final.

There are different ways to combine ideas in sentences. Here are two examples:

- *Interviewed after the incident, Gaius's manager admitted he was angry with his rider.*
  Here, the subordinate clause is placed before the main clause, separated by a comma. It explains when the manager said these things. The writer has used a temporal link (*after*).

- *My fans are the most loyal in the world, and if my manager has me whipped he'll have all the windows in his town house broken in the middle of the night...*
  This sentence has three clauses. Here, the writer has used *if... [then]* to link the second and third clauses, with a simple *and* for the first link.

Complex sentences (2) – clauses

The purpose of this unit is to revise and develop pupils' understanding of complex sentences.

NLS coverage

Key objective

SL 5 To form complex sentences through reading back complex sentences for clarity of meaning, adjusting as necessary; exploring how meaning is affected by the sequence and structure of clauses

Learned through:

TL Reading comprehension and writing composition
12, 13, 17 To comment critically on the language, style and success of non-fiction texts; to secure understanding of the features of non-chronological reports; to write non-chronological reports

Assessment criteria

SL By the end of this unit, pupils should be able to:
- form complex sentences
- manipulate sentences by altering the sequence of clauses
- select the most appropriate sentence structure for their purpose.

TL Writing composition
Children should be able to write non-chronological reports.

Session 1

You will need OHT 6 and PCM 6A.

Shared reading

1 Explain to pupils that you will be reading a report about Liverpool. Allow two or three minutes for them to discuss what they know about the city. Share these facts; construct a concept map about Liverpool, linking ideas as pupils express them.

2 Display and read OHT 6. How many new facts have they learned? Count these.

3 Look at the structure of the report. Focus on the number of paragraphs, and the subject of each. Ask pupils to compose a heading for each paragraph.

4 Discuss the text. Was it easy to read? Who might be interested in reading a text such as this?

Sentence level work

1 To get ideas across as succinctly as possible, the writer has used a number of complex sentences. S/he has had to decide how to put the sentences together, the order in which to present clauses, etc. This is one way in which spoken and written language differ – writers can play about with sentences until they are satisfied with them.

Speakers don't have enough time to do this.

2 Explain that you are going to look closely at the way in which the writer has put these complex sentences together. Begin by looking at the second sentence from the first paragraph:
Originally granted a charter by King John in 1207, it had become one of England's most prosperous ports by the nineteenth century.
How many clauses are there in this sentence? (Two)
If pupils find this difficult, remind them that each clause has a verb phrase, and that clauses are often separated by commas. Highlight the two clauses in different colours so pupils can see where the division is.

3 Try breaking the complex sentence down into two separate sentences.
Liverpool was originally granted a charter by King John in 1207. It had become one of England's most prosperous ports by the nineteenth century.
Note that the subject of the sentence is carried over from the previous sentence – this is one way in which the writer has linked the sentences. Experiment with different ways of putting these sentences together. For example:
Although it had become one of England's most prosperous ports by the nineteenth century, Liverpool was originally granted a charter by King John in 1207.

4 Look at the difference between the three versions of this sentence. Look at the different emphasis in

each. Does any of these variations give the impression of a rapidly growing town? Which is the most interesting sentence? Which version would be easiest for younger children to understand?

5 Follow the same process with the final sentence in the second paragraph.

Independent activities

Direct pupils to PCM 6A which asks them to practise this process.

Plenary

Compare pupils' sentences. How many variations are there for each pair? Which are the most successful? Encourage pupils to verbalize their reasons.

Session 2

You will need pupils' book 4, Unit 6, pages 20–21.

Shared reading

1 Explain that you will be reading another report about an area – the island of Anglesey in Wales. If any pupils know the island well, discuss what might be included in the report. Locate Anglesey on a map.

2 Ask pupils to turn to the text in the pupils' book, and allow them five minutes to read it and extract five facts about Anglesey from the text.

3 Share the facts pupils have collected. Discuss which have been selected by most pupils and why, e.g. they relate to pupils' own interests.

4 Explain to pupils that this text is in the style of a tourist guide. Is it successful in describing Anglesey's attractions to people of their age? What additional questions do they have? What other information would be useful? (e.g. opening times, admission charges, etc.)

5 Pupils may want to try and pronounce the name of Llanfairpwllgwyngyllgogerychwyrndrobwllllantysilio-gogogoch. Teach them yourself, using a tape if necessary.

Sentence level work

1 Remind pupils that you are working on the sequence of clauses in sentences. Select one sentence, and swap around the clauses, e.g.
*Covering 276 square miles, **Anglesey** is the largest island in Wales and England.*

Anglesey is the largest island in Wales and England, covering 276 square miles.

2 Discuss these sentences. Do pupils prefer one over the other? Does it make a great deal of difference?

3 Some of the sentences in this text contain more than two clauses. Experiment with altering the sequence of clauses in these sentences:
It has been connected with the mainland since 1826, when Thomas Telford built the Menai Bridge, the first heavy-duty suspension bridge to be constructed.
The first heavy-duty suspension bridge ever constructed was built by Thomas Telford in 1826 to connect Anglesey with the mainland.

4 Can pupils spot which piece of information has been omitted from the second sentence? (the name of the bridge) Consider other alternatives, e.g. *The first heavy-duty suspension bridge ever constructed was the Menai Bridge which connects Anglesey with the mainland.*

5 Notice how both rewritten sentences shift the emphasis to the bridge rather than Anglesey, which is the subject of the text. Consider other ways of combining this information into one sentence.

Independent activities

Children complete questions A and B in the pupils' book.

Plenary

Discuss which sentences were easiest to rewrite. Invite pupils to state which sentence was most different when rewritten. Share these sentences and see if others agree.

Session 3

You will need OHT 6, pupils' book 4, Unit 6, pages 20–21, PCM 6B, and the Reminder Sheet.

Shared writing

Explain that you will be working on a guide for visitors to the local area. Refer to the model texts, and look at the way they are constructed. You may find it helpful to revisit the headings pupils selected for OHT 6. Pupils should notice that the texts begin with some geographical and/or historical information, and then go on to describe aspects which might interest visitors. The text may then have a conclusion. Identify these parts in the reports you have read.

Write together

1 Photocopy PCM 6B onto OHT. Ask pupils to generate ideas for each section of the report.

2 Once each section is full, discuss whether all information should be included, or if any additional information is required.

3 Now look at the first paragraph, and decide on the sequence in which information should be presented. Number the items accordingly.

Independent writing activity

Pupils research information about their area, and record it onto PCM 6B. Support pupils who may have difficulty with locating or sequencing information.

Plenary

Remind pupils that they may have additional resources at home – including parents/carers! – to help plug any gaps. Allow time for them to complete and exchange plans with a partner to check that all necessary information has been included.

Session 4

You will need pupils' book 4, Unit 6, pages 20–21, PCM 6B, and the Reminder Sheet.

Shared writing

Revisit the plan from the previous session. Check that pupils are still happy with the content of the piece.

Write together

Begin to write the notes into prose. Demonstrate sentence construction as you write, experimenting with different ways of putting sentences together and asking pupils for input. Take this opportunity to revise connectives.

Independent writing activity

Pupils complete their own reports. Work with groups, selecting sentences from their reports and discussing options for reconstructing them.

Plenary

1 Revisit the shared writing. Discuss options for presentation, e.g. use of diagrams/maps/photographs. Consider layout.

2 Allow pupils to complete and present their 'tourist guides' in IT sessions, or as homework.

Assessment

Comment upon the extent to which pupils have:
• structured the report appropriately
• used complex sentences
• varied the structure of sentences.
In guided sessions, discuss sentence construction.
Note pupils' understanding of terminology.

Model answers

Pupils' book 4 ☐ **A**

1 Pupils should mention farming and tourism.
2 It provides a lot of food from farming for the rest of Wales.
3 Pupils should mention how it might help attract tourists.
4 Because it is so old, well built, famous, well-preserved.
5 Answers will vary.

Pupils' book 4 ☐ **B**

Answers will vary; this is a rough guide:

6 a) *Although there are some rugged cliffs around the coast, Anglesey is the flattest part of Wales.*

   b) *The island provides wheat, cattle and other farm produce for North Wales, and so is referred to as Mon Mam Cymru – Mother of Wales.*

   c) *They'll teach you how to pronounce it at the Tourist Information Centre in the knitwear shop near the station.*

☐ **6A and 6B**   Complex sentences (2) – clauses ▯
Answers will vary.

Clauses in sentences

Here are pairs of sentences about Liverpool. Try to combine each pair into one sentence in different ways. When you have done this, read all of the sentences and put a tick by the one you think works best. Remember to vary the order of the clauses.

1	Liverpool lies on the River Mersey.	Liverpool is west of Manchester.
	a)	
	b)	
	c)	
2	Liverpool is famous for its music.	Many comedians come from Liverpool.
	a)	
	b)	
	c)	
3	Liverpool has many beautiful parks.	Sefton Park is the largest park in Liverpool.
	a)	
	b)	
	c)	
4	Speke Hall is a Tudor house in Liverpool.	The Norris family of Speke were one of the great Liverpool families.
	a)	
	b)	
	c)	

Complex sentences (2) – clauses

My favourite place

This is a planning frame for a report on a geographical area. Make a note of the information you will need to include in each paragraph, and use this as the basis for your report.

Description: size / location / interesting features

History: when first named / main industries, etc.

Item of interest 1: historical site / visitor centre / attraction

Item of interest 2: historical site / visitor centre / attraction

Conclusion:

In complex sentences, the writer decides in which order clauses should be presented. This can change the emphasis of the sentence. For example:

> Anglesey has been connected with the mainland since 1826, when Thomas Telford built the Menai Bridge, the first heavy-duty suspension bridge to be constructed.

> The first heavy-duty suspension bridge was the Menai Bridge, built by Thomas Telford in 1826, which connected Anglesey with the mainland.

Although both sentences contain the same information, the first seems to have come from a text about Anglesey while the other seems to have come from a text about bridges.

When you are writing, think about the order in which you write clauses. In your head, try different ways of ordering the information, and then choose the one that seems best.

Punctuation

The purpose of this unit is to develop pupils' ability to punctuate complex sentences.

NLS coverage

Key objective

SL **6** To secure knowledge and understanding of more sophisticated punctuation marks: colon; semi-colon; parenthetic commas, dashes, brackets

Learned through:

TL **Reading comprehension and writing composition**
12, 13, 17 To comment critically on the language, style and success of non-fiction texts; to secure understanding of the features of non-chronological reports; to write non-chronological reports

Assessment criteria

SL By the end of this unit, pupils should be able to:
■ identify and name punctuation marks
■ read texts with expression appropriate to punctuation
■ explain why writers have chosen particular punctuation
■ use these punctuation marks with increasing accuracy.

TL **Writing composition**
Children should be able to write a report on a topic.

Session 1

You will need OHT 7 and PCM 7A; first section of Reminder Sheet 7 copied onto OHT.

Shared reading

1 Introduce the topic by asking pupils what they know about plants. Discuss briefly – why is the study of plants important? How might it be useful to pupils in their lives now, or in the future?

2 Display and read OHT 7. Is the material existing knowledge, or is any of it new to pupils? Discuss how it relates to their own hands-on knowledge, e.g. of weed for fish tanks, cacti. What is the most interesting information in the text?

3 Discuss how user-friendly the text is. At what age-group is it aimed? Why? Is the language accessible? Consider vocabulary, sentence length and other factors related to readability. How might this be improved? Consider how adding diagrams or photographs may help readers.

Sentence level work

1 Explain that you will be reviewing punctuation. Remove the OHT and ask pupils to list the punctuation marks they remember. Ask if there are any that were definitely not used (e.g. speech marks). Write up a list of the marks pupils think were used. Ask them to explain the purpose of each, and record this next to the marks.

2 Now review the text and see if pupils were correct.

3 Check on the writer's use of punctuation. Have the marks been used in accordance with pupils' recall of their purposes?

4 Display the first section of the Reminder Sheet on OHT and compare with pupils' own list of the purposes of punctuation marks. Discuss any differences, and check once more that the writer has used punctuation accurately. Where alternatives are given for functions of punctuation marks, can pupils identify which is which? It may be useful to make this available to pupils during the independent activity – either on OHT or as individual photocopies.

Independent activities

1 Ask pupils to identify one of the punctuation marks with which they are not yet confident. Some may still be struggling with basic sentence punctuation; others will wish to work on semi-colons, etc. Group pupils according to their choice, and your assessment of their progress. Explain that they will

be reviewing their last piece of extended writing, or one on which they are working, and altering punctuation as necessary. PCM 7A will enable them to record alterations.

2 Identify a group of pupils who have not quite gained control of one of these punctuation marks, and support them as they work. Pupils could transfer one sentence each onto an OHT version of PCM 7A for the plenary.

Plenary

Ask pupils you have been supporting to share their work. Discuss how the changes have improved the sentences, and the impact they have had on the whole piece.

Session 2

You will need pupils' book 4, Unit 7, pages 22–3, Reminder Sheet 7, and a selection of non-fiction texts.

Shared reading

1 Explain to pupils that you will be learning more about a particular group of plants, called 'parasites'. Does any pupil know what this word means?

2 Read the extract from the pupils' book. Discuss why parasites may be useful in nature (e.g. they may be a source of food for other creatures, or limit the growth of the host).

3 Ask pupils to list the ways in which parasitic plants may be different from other plants, from what they have read in the text. How much have they learned from the text? If they had to pick one new fact to tell their families, which one would they pick?

Sentence level work

1 Explain that you will be looking at 'parenthesis'. This is a term which is used to describe extra detail writers insert into the middle of sentences. Ask pupils if they can find examples in the text of parenthetic constructions. They may find:

Some plants, such as mistletoe, are only partly parasitic, and are known as 'hemiparasites'.

Each flower weighs nearly 7kg (15lb) and reaches up to 1m (3ft) in diameter.

These are insects which bite other animals – including humans – and use their blood as food.

2 Identify the information which is inserted. Invite pupils to read the sentences with these insertions,

and then without. Consider the way they use their voices to indicate parenthesis in speech.

3 There are three ways of marking parenthesis used here – commas, dashes and brackets. Practise constructing sentences using parenthesis. Create these orally, and then write them down. Are there differences between the punctuation marks? Refer pupils to the second section of the Reminder Sheet.

4 Discuss which works best in which situation. Which is the strongest – i.e. which separates most firmly? Also consider the length of insertions. Distribute other texts so pupils can look for examples.

Independent activities

Children complete questions A and B in the pupils' book.

Plenary

Pupils share examples found in other texts. Discuss again the word 'parasite'. Consider other words that have the prefix *para*, e.g. *paragraph, paratrooper, paradise, paralyse.* Can pupils think of any link between these words? If so, is any word an 'odd one out'?

Session 3

You will need pupils' book 4, Unit 7, pages 22–3, and the Reminder Sheet.

Shared writing

1 Explain to pupils that you will be writing a report about plants, using what you already knew about them, what you have learned from the texts you have read, and additional information included on PCM 7B. As a class, you will generate and organize facts for the report. Pupils will then write their individual versions, including information from PCM 7B and any other additional facts they know.

2 Begin by asking pupils to review the facts they offered at the beginning of the unit. Record these. Ask pupils to offer information about plants that they have learned from the texts, or from other sources. Remind them that some of the information, e.g. about human parasites, is not relevant.

3 Once pupils have 'run dry', prompt if there is anything major omitted, then go on to look at how the information may be organized, using a concept map if pupils are familiar with this technique.

4 Now select the general classification information you will use for the opening of the report. Go on to identify (perhaps with numbers) the sequence in which information will be presented.

Write together

Begin by composing the opening and second paragraphs. Be explicit about use of punctuation. Refer to the Reminder Sheet, and invite pupils' opinions.

Independent writing activity

Pupils complete the draft of the basic report, referring back to the concept map or similar document. Encourage pupils to write on alternate lines so that they have plenty of space for adding information.

Plenary

Discuss progress on the text. Is anything omitted? Is any part of the text less detailed? Do pupils feel they needed additional information about any aspect of the topic? Explain that some of this will be supplied by PCM 7B. They may, however, wish to carry out some research of their own before the next session.

Session 4

You will need pupils' book 4, Unit 7, pages 22–3, PCM 7B, and the Reminder Sheet.

Shared writing

Return to the writing from the previous session. Ask pupils if they have found any additional information relevant to this writing. Take contributions.

Write together

1 Model inserting this information, using parenthetic devices investigated in Session 2. Experiment with alternative constructions and devices until pupils feel that the sentence is satisfactory.

2 Distribute PCM 7B and read it through with pupils.

Independent writing activity

Pupils continue writing, inserting additional information. Offer support to pupils who may struggle with the task.

Plenary

Pupils share reports with a partner, and select a section to read to the rest of the class.

Assessment

• In discussion, check on pupils' ability to identify and name punctuation marks from reading.
• Comment on the extent to which pupils have used punctuation within sentences appropriately.
• Focus on the progress of pupils, rather than the number of different punctuation marks used; some pupils may still be struggling with basic sentence punctuation or use of commas and their progress should also be commended.
• Challenge pupils to demonstrate use of their new knowledge in their next piece of writing.
• Reinforce text organization, and the way in which pupils have sequenced and linked points.

Model answers

Pupils' book 4 ◺ **A**

1 Because they don't make their own food, like most other plants. Pupils may think of their own names. If pupils are struggling, suggest they use a thesaurus.

2 Answers will vary. Pupils may suggest that the host plants would be weakened.

3 Answers will vary.

4 People don't like parasites which affect them – like fleas and lice. Pupils may also suggest an emotional response to the idea of a parasite.

5 Answers will vary. Pupils should identify the link between the word and the concepts of laziness, stealing.

Pupils' book 4 ◺ **B**

6 Answers will vary.

7 The writer has used inverted commas to identify a word which is being discussed/defined.

◺ **7A Improving punctuation** ▯

Answers will vary.

7A *Improving punctuation*

Select a piece of your own writing. Decide which punctuation mark you are going to put in. Then read your work and look for places where you might use this punctuation mark. You might have to change the word order, or even take out some words.

I am going to use a new punctuation mark	Comma Colon Semi-colon

Original wording	New sentence	How the new sentence is better

Here is some additional information on plants.

More about plants

Papyrus is a reed (water plant) that can grow up to 3 metres high. The first paper was made by ancient Egyptians from papyrus.

Many plants growing in cold climates have fine hairs on their stems and leaves which help to insulate the plant. Examples of such plants are: mountain kidney vetch and rock roses.

In order to withstand drought, succulent plants often have waxy leaves which stop water being lost from the surface of the leaf.

Plants which grow in deserts sometimes have leaves which are furry. This protects them from the sun in the day and the cold at night.

Some plants live on others without being parasites. Many of these plants simply grow on larger plants and trees so that they can reach the sunlight.

Punctuation mark	Function
comma	a) separates parts of sentences, such as clauses b) encloses additional information
semi-colon	a) separates items in a list if the items are one word or more b) links clauses which are really separate sentences
colon	a) introduces lists, including lists of examples b) introduces an explanation or the expansion of a point

Parenthetic device	Function
commas – pairs	Pairs of commas can be used to insert additional information, or to clarify meaning, e.g. *My dog Suki is brown. (I have lots of dogs.)* *My dog, Suki, is brown. (I have one dog.)*
brackets – pairs	Pairs of round brackets are used to separate off information which is not essential to the sentence, e.g. *Each sack weighs 7kg (15lb).*
dashes – pairs	Pairs of dashes can be used to separate information, but are not as strong as brackets, e.g. *The driver – Peter Assan – ran for the door.*

Test preparation (1) – writing stylish scenes

The purpose of this unit is to focus upon style and punctuation as part of preparation for national tests. It links all the previous work on words and sentences and punctuation. It is linked to unit 9 which looks at relating the task to the features required.

NLS coverage

Key objective

[SL] To revise all that has been covered about words, sentences and punctuation in preparation for national tests, with a particular focus on securing level 4 or better, rather than level 3.

Learned through:

[TL] Writing composition
To write a scene from a story, using at least the required features to attain level 4.

Assessment criteria

[SL] By the end of this unit, pupils will have revised the following:
- punctuation, notably accurate use of speech marks and commas
- use of effective vocabulary
- varying sentences for effect – short, long, simple, compound, complex, question/exclamation.

[TL] Writing composition
Children will have revised the ability to write a short scene, using the required stylistic features for level 4, or above.

Session 1

You will need OHT 8 and PCM 8A.

Shared reading

1 Display OHT 8. Is this a good piece of writing?

2 First, improve it by working on the words and sentences. Try the following:
- improve the verbs – *got, went, said, walked, looked*
- add in extra description – using adjectives
- vary some of the sentence openings
- use a question and an exclamation
- use a simile.

Sentence level work

Second, work on the punctuation. Ask pupils to:
- find where full stops and capital letters are needed
- check the speech
- check for apostrophes in shortened words, e.g. *can't*.

Independent activities

Direct pupils to PCM 8A. Having worked on improving the opening to the story, the class now have to rewrite the ending. They should make sure that the sentences are improved, the vocabulary enhanced and accuracy achieved. They need to add in more description and suggest how characters are feeling. The final paragraph needs a scene to itself.

Plenary

Listen to several examples and draw attention to well written sentences and paragraphs.

Session 2

You will need pupils' book 4, Unit 8, pages 24–5, and PCM 8B.

Shared reading

1 It is worth marking pupils' work using the current national mark scheme. Respond to their improvements on the PCM from the previous lesson. Make it clear what was successful and what they have to do to secure the next level up. This could be written as 'Next time…'

2 Read through the extract from *Cirque Du Freak*. What type of story is this from – and how do you know?

Sentence level work

1 Which words or phrases help to create a frightening atmosphere? (*dark, cold, freezing, scratched*)

2 Which is the most descriptive sentence?

3 Which creates the most tension?

Independent activities

Children complete questions A and B in the pupils' book. Use PCM 8B to improve another level 3 piece of writing. Children should bear in mind your suggestions for 'next time'.

Plenary

Use the plenary to reread the extract and make a checklist of different devices that the writer uses. Listen to different strategies for improving the PCM writing. Demonstrate how to improve a string of dialogue by thinking about:
- what the speaker does
- what the listener does
- anything else going on. For example:

'Get it Jason,' shouted Tim, waving to his friend. Jason glanced back.

'OK, Tim,' he called, rushing towards where the ball had landed. Tim waited patiently.

'Have you found it?' added Solly, joining the gang. They all stared to where Jason was poking the grass.

'Yes, but it's got a puncture,' came his voice, drifting across the playground. …

Session 3

You will need pupils' book 4, Unit 8, pages 24–5, and the Reminder Sheet.

Shared writing

Explain that the task in question 7 is to use the same basic structure to write a similar passage. Revisit the checklist. Remind pupils of the need to ensure:
- accurate punctuation, with speech marks and commas correctly used
- effective vocabulary
- a variety of sentences – short, long, simple, compound, complex, question/exclamation.

Box the scenes so that the sequence is quite clear.

Write together

1 Demonstrate the opening and then involve the children. Ask them to write their suggestions for sentences on whiteboards. Before they show their ideas they must check for sense, quality and accuracy.
We found ourselves standing in an old yard. A horse stood silent in the corner. Otherwise it was quite empty and quiet. Solly grabbed the door and pushed. It gave an agonizing squeak that sounded like a gunshot. We slipped in like ferrets down a rabbit's hole. And stood in pitch darkness…

2 Keep referring back to the model and to the checklist. Direct them to the Reminder Sheet.

Independent writing activity

The children write their own version, having decided the names of their characters, where they are, and what they are looking for. Remind them of the 'next time' targets before, during and after writing.

Plenary

Listen to examples. See if the author, and then class, can identify potential places for improvement.

Session 4

You will need a section of work you have written, or one written by a pupil, on OHT, and the Reminder Sheet.

Shared writing

Remind pupils of the focus – writing a scary scene, ensuring:

- accurate punctuation, with speech marks and commas correctly used
- effective vocabulary
- a variety of sentences for effect – short, long, simple, compound, complex, question/exclamation.

Write together

Revise, as a class, a version that contains any typical weaknesses.

Independent writing activity

Allow a brief time for very swift, focused revision.

Plenary

Pairs review their writing and targets.

Assessment

Sentence level
Pupils should be able to:

- use punctuation accurately, notably speech marks and commas
- use effective vocabulary
- vary sentences for effect – short, long, simple, compound, complex, question/exclamation.

Writing composition
Children should be able to write a short scene, using the required stylistic features for level 4 or above.

Model answers

Pupils' book 4 ☐ A

1 The main character is scared, his nerves are on edge (*I was glad of that; I almost turned and ran; we nearly jumped out of our skins*). Steve is calm and confident to begin with: he gives a practical reason for the coldness, opens the door, shows no fear, etc.

2 By emphasizing the darkness and cold, the squalor of the house, the time of the visit; by likening the sound of a creaking door to the noise of *the lid of a coffin being tugged open!*

3 He gives a normal, reassuring reason for the coldness.

4 Maybe they were dry with fear.

Pupils' book 4 ☐ B

5 Answers will vary.

6 Not really – it's the description that creates the atmosphere, rather than the author just telling the reader that it was scary.

8A   Test preparation (1) – writing stylish scenes
Ensure the writing uses more effective vocabulary, description, varied sentences and accurate punctuation, e.g. *'Help,' she screamed, struggling to stay afloat. At that moment, Joe ambled down the deserted canal path…*

8B   Test preparation (1) – writing stylish scenes
Check for improvement and accuracy, as well as description to split up the dialogue, e.g.
We were all hanging about in the playground. Miss had told us that we could play football. I passed to Jason and he kicked it hard. We watched it sail over the fence.
'Get it Jason,' groaned Tim, hands on his hips. Jason shrugged and looked over the fence. The ball had landed in the road.
'OK, Tim,' replied Jason…

8A Test preparation (1) – writing stylish scenes

Improve the end of the story, printed below. You may need to add in extra sentences and extend paragraphs. Make sure you use:

- better words
- more description
- varied sentences
- accurate punctuation.

'Help,' she screamed. Just at that moment someone came down the path. It was Joe. Joe was her best friend from school. He saw Sasha in the canal.

'I'll get you,' said Joe. He got a long pole and Sasha got the end. He pulled and pulled and soon Sasha was on the bank. She was puffing and she was wet.

Joe took Sasha home. She got grounded for a week.

_____

_____

_____

_____

_____

_____

_____

_____

_____

_____

_____

_____

Rewrite this passage improving it and making the punctuation accurate. You will need to improve the dialogue, shortening it and putting description in between what is said.

We was all in the playground. Miss said that we could play football. We got the ball and kicked it it went out

'get it Jason.'

'OK Tim.

Have you

Yes

OK

They had got it they went to the park for a game.

_____

_____

_____

_____

_____

_____

_____

_____

_____

_____

_____

When writing, think about the following:

1 Work out roughly what is going to happen before you write.

2 Use effective vocabulary – precise nouns, well-chosen adjectives, powerful verbs.

3 Use some stylistic effects, e.g. similes, personification, alliteration.

4 Make sure you have some descriptive sentences.

5 Check that you have stuck in the same tense.

6 Avoid a string of speech – fill in between what is said by thinking about what the speaker does, what the listener does, and what else is happening.

7 Create some characterization – show what a character thinks and feels through what they say (how they say it), what they do, and what others think of them.

8 Add in extra detail for interest.

9 Have a strong ending.

10 Vary your sentences for effect – short, long, simple, compound, complex, question/exclamation.

11 Punctuate your sentences accurately; use speech marks, commas, question marks and exclamation marks correctly.

Test preparation (2)
– writing stylish scenes

The purpose of this unit is to focus on style and punctuation, identifying from a set question what type of writing and features are required.
It links all the previous work on words, sentences and punctuation, and to Unit 8 which focuses more on written style.

NLS coverage

Key objective

[SL] To revise all that has been covered about words, sentences and punctuation in preparation for national tests, with a particular focus on securing level 4 or better, rather than level 3.

Learned through:

[TL] To identify the nature of a set writing task, and consider what type of writing is needed, with what particular features; to write a scene from a story, using at least the required features to attain level 4.

Assessment criteria

[SL] By the end of this unit, pupils will have revised the following:
- punctuation, including accurate use of speech marks and commas
- use of speech to make characters distinct
- varying sentences for effect – short, long, simple, compound, complex, question/exclamation.

[TL] Writing composition
Children will be have revised the ability to write a short scene, using the required stylistic features for level 4, as well as plan the type of writing needed to address a set question.

Session 1

You will need OHT 9 and PCM 9A.

Shared reading

Display OHT 9 and discuss each question in turn. For example, for question 1: What type of writing is this? What sort of structure will be needed? Create a simple plan, e.g.
- *Hello to old friend – missing you*
- *Good things about the new school (good library, learning French, etc.)*
- *A great day – theatre trip (I love theatre / want to be an actress)*
- *Missing old teacher, friends, playing netball, etc.*
- *Let's meet up*
- *Do write to me – goodbye.*

Emphasize the need for balance to be given to each part of the writing.

Sentence level work

What language features might be needed? For example:
- typical words and phrases
- useful connectives
- sentence types
- punctuation
- other features, such as bullet points.

Independent activities

Direct pupils to PCM 9A. Look at the two questions. Complete the grid. Write the opening. Discuss the need to use the right sort of language.

Plenary

Go over the children's ideas and listen to several examples. Emphasize that it needs to sound right – to sound like the sort of writing that they are trying to emulate.

Session 2

You will need pupils' book 4, Unit 9, pages 26–7, and PCM 9B.

Shared reading

Read the passage through and take first reactions. Is 'The Crumbles' easy to find? Why does Skater show it to Zip? What do you think it means to Skater? What sort of boy do you think Skater is? What might have triggered the memory of Zip's mum?

Sentence level work

1 How is the speech made distinctive?

2 Focus on the way in which description is used to show the reader what is happening while the dialogue is going on. For instance, the writer could have written:

   ''ere Zip, wanna come down the Crumbles?' he said. 'Where's that then?' I asked.

3 Which is the best written sentence?

4 Justify the choice.

Independent activities

Children complete questions A and B in the pupils' book. Use PCM 9B to practise improving dialogue.

Plenary

Use the plenary to go over the answers and to hear how the dialogue has been improved.

Session 3

You will need pupils' book 4, Unit 9, pages 26–7, and the Reminder Sheet.

Shared writing

1 Reread the passage. Explain that the task in question 6 is to use the same basic structure and storyline to write a similar passage.

2 Draw attention to the need for:
   - accurate punctuation, with speech marks and commas correctly used
   - effective vocabulary – description, detail, similes
   - speech to make characters distinct, avoiding a stream of dialogue
   - interesting action
   - varied sentences – short, long, simple, compound, complex, question/exclamation.

Write together

Demonstrate and then involve the class. For example:
Spud just looked at me. 'You want to go to the old house?' I shuffled my feet nervously. He was bigger than me and known to have a temper.
'Yep, if it's ok by you,' I stammered. He shrugged his shoulders and grunted. I thought that I detected a 'yes' and followed him.
We made our way down the snicket, and into Jigger's Yard. He grinned at me and pulled out an old bacon sandwich. 'Here,' he said. 'You'd better take a bite afore we gets in.'

Independent writing activity

The children write their own version, having decided on the names of the two characters, where they are going and what will be there. Just before writing, remind them of their targets and direct them to the Reminder Sheet.

Plenary

Listen to their versions and comment, especially where dialogue is well handled.

Session 4

You will need a section of work you have written, or one written by a pupil, on OHT, and the Reminder Sheet.

Shared writing

Remind pupils of the focus – writing an interesting scene, varying their use of language.

Write together

Focus on several that are OK but with a little extra effort could be good. Improve the use of language, add in stylistic effects such as simile, vary sentences, use detail and characterization. Make the speech distinctive.

Independent writing activity

Children revise their writing.

Plenary

Listen to good examples where pupils feel that their writing has improved.

Assessment

Sentence level
Pupils should be able to:
- use accurate punctuation, including speech marks and commas
- use effective vocabulary – for description and detail; similes
- use speech to make characters distinct
- use powerful verbs to write action scenes
- vary sentences for effect – short, long, simple, compound, complex, question/exclamation
- paragraph scenes.

Writing composition
Children will have revised the ability to write a short scene, using the required stylistic features for level 4, as well as plan the type of writing needed to address a set question.

Model answers

Pupils' book 4 ☐ A

1 Answers will vary, e.g. Zip has saved Skater's dog; Skater is lonely and wants a friend; Skater wants to share his secret place with someone; Skater's Nan knows Zip's Mum is ill and wants Skater to tell Zip that she'll be OK; Skater feels sorry for Zip.

2 He's not sure how to take Skater, and he's worried about his Mum being ill.

3 By telling him that his Nan says that Zip's Mum will be OK.

4 He doesn't like to show his feelings.

Pupils' book 4 ☐ B

5 Answers will vary.

☐ **9A**   Test preparation (2) – writing stylish scenes ▯
Check the plans include: an opening, a paragraph for each section, an ending. Ensure that the children are thinking about the type of writing, its purpose and audience, and how this affects the style.

☐ **9B**   Test preparation (2) – writing stylish scenes ▯
Answers will vary, e.g. *'Your family don't care what happens to you,' smirked Jan, as she flicked back her hair. Rubina gasped – she couldn't believe what she had heard. Billy Jo knew that Jan was being unkind but didn't dare say anything. At that moment, the school bell rang. Rubina straightened up, held her head high and replied, 'At least I know the difference between right and wrong.'*…

Test preparation (2) – writing stylish scenes

Look at the two questions and choose one. Write a rough paragraph guide. Make notes to address the points on the grid. Then write, at least, the opening.

EITHER

Write a newspaper report based on the rhyme 'Humpty Dumpty'.

You should think about the following:

■ details of Humpty's life
■ what happened
■ an interview with an observer
■ the paper's own comment.

OR

Write a report for new parents about the school and what it has to offer.

You will need to include:

■ basic facts about the school
■ the main strengths of the school
■ other advantages
■ how to make an appointment to look round.

Copy this grid into your book, leaving plenty of space for your notes.

typical words and phrases:
possible useful connectives:
sentence ideas:
punctuation:
other features, e.g. bullet points:

Test preparation (2) – writing stylish scenes

The dialogue in the speech bubbles is rather dull. Improve it by writing down what happens in between. You could mention:

- What the speaker (Jan) does (*She picked up her hair grip and flicked back her hair.*)

- What the listener (Rubina) does (*Rubina's eyes filled with tears.*)

- What someone is thinking (*Billy Jo thought that Jan had been too hard on Rubina. It wasn't her fault, after all.*)

- What else happens (*There was a knock at the door and they could hear Mrs Wartalski chatting to the postman.*)

9 Test preparation (2) – writing stylish scenes

Think about the writing task

The first questions to ask are – who is this for and what is its purpose?

Then think about the type, or types, of writing needed.

Make a rough plan, including some sort of opening and ending.

Make notes of any:
- useful words and phrases
- appropriate connectives
- sentence ideas
- specific punctuation
- other features, e.g. bullet points.

In your writing you need:

- Accurate punctuation, with speech marks and commas correctly used.
- Effective and appropriate vocabulary – description, detail, similes, powerful language, formal or informal, relevant connectives, etc.
- Interesting action, description, detail, information, humour and ideas.
- Varied sentences to create interest, rhythm and impact – short, long, simple, compound, complex, question/exclamation.

When writing dialogue:

1 Try to make your characters special by giving them an expression only they use, a local accent, local words and phrases.

2 Think about how the character feels or what sort of person they are – then decide what they would say.

3 Use a powerful speech verb, or an adverb or plain 'said'.

4 Avoid a string of speech.

5 Write what happens as characters talk, filling in between what is said. For example, think about:
- What the speaker does (*She picked up her hair grip and flicked back her hair.*)
- What the listener does (*Rubina's eyes filled with tears.*)
- What someone is thinking (*Billy Jo thought that Jan had been too hard on Rubina. It wasn't her fault, after all.*)
- What else happens (*There was a knock at the door and they could hear Mrs Wartalski chatting to the postman.*)

Who dunnit?

The purpose of this unit is to deepen children's understanding of active and passive verbs. It links to work carried out in term 1.

NLS coverage

Key objective

SL 1 To investigate further the use of active and passive verbs:
- secure the use of the terms 'active' and 'passive'
- know how sentences can be reordered by changing from one to another
- identify examples of active and passive verbs in texts
- experiment in transformation from active to passive and vice-versa, and study the impact of this on meaning
- consider how the passive voice can conceal the agent of a sentence

Learned through:

TL Writing composition
10 To use different genres as models to write, e.g. an invented recount

Assessment criteria

SL By the end of this unit, pupils should be able to identify and discuss the use of active and passive; transform one to the other.

TL Writing composition
Children should be able to use the passive voice to 'hide' the subject/perpetrator in a short piece of writing.

Session 1

You will need OHT 10 and PCM 10A.

Shared reading

1 Display OHT 10 and read through each sentence one by one.
2 Play 'Who dunnit?' and work out the answer to each one.

Sentence level work

1 What is similar about all the sentences? Who can explain?
2 Remind the class about the passive voice.
3 Now convert each sentence back into active, for example:
   - *A glass slipper has been left behind after the palace ball* becomes *Cinderella left behind a glass slipper after the palace ball.*
   - *Three bowls of porridge were eaten* becomes *Goldilocks ate three bowls of porridge.*

Independent activities

Direct pupils to PCM 10A. Pupils have to identify which sentences are active and which are passive. They then transform each sentence from one to the other to reveal or hide 'who dunnit'. You may need to demonstrate how to tackle the first two.

Plenary

Check how successful the transformations have been. Have pupils been able to hide or reveal the criminals?

Session 2

You will need pupils' book 4, Unit 10, pages 28–9, and PCM 10B.

Shared reading

1 Read and discuss the story, taking first impressions.
2 What type of story is this?

3 What age group might enjoy it – why would it be suitable?

4 Describe the basic pattern.

Sentence level work

1 Find an active sentence in the story.

2 Find a passive sentence (look for one that could have *'by....'* tagged on the end).

3 Change this passive sentence into active: *Her coat was ripped.* You will have to decide 'who dunnit'.

Independent activities

Children complete questions A and B in the pupils' book. Use PCM 10B to identify and transform a set of headlines.

Plenary

Use the plenary to go over the questions and PCM 10B.

Session 3

You will need pupils' book 4, Unit 10, pages 28–9, and the Reminder Sheet.

Shared writing

Explain the task in question 8 – to use the same sort of repetitive structure, and passive voice, to write in a similar way about a disastrous school trip.

Write together
Demonstrate and then involve the pupils. For example:
Class 6 arrived at 'The Fun Park'. They rushed straight in, whooping and yelling. Poor Mr Hadenough, their weary teacher, followed on behind. The only other visitor was Mr Revenge, an off-duty school inspector.
First they went on the bouncy castle. Darren's shoes were stolen. Mr Hadenough sat on a park bench and dozed.
Then they went on the water chute. Daisy's clothes were soaked. Mr Hadenough waited on the grass.
After that...

Independent writing activity

Children write their own version, sticking to the same sort of pattern.

Plenary

Pupils practise reading their narratives in pairs, followed by a presentation in which a few read aloud to entertain the class. The best could be voted upon to visit another class with their tale.

Session 4

You will need a section of work you have written, or one written by a pupil, on OHT, and the Reminder Sheet.

Shared writing

Remind pupils of the focus – writing a patterned tale using the passive voice to hide the perpetrator.

Write together
Look at successful examples. Work as a class on weaker examples, especially sorting out the passive voice.

Independent writing activity

Pupils revise their narratives and then improve their presentation, so that they can read to another class!

Plenary

Listen and vote, after discussing what makes a good reading aloud – clarity, varying expression, volume, pace and tone, etc.

Assessment

Sentence level
Pupils should be able to:
• identify and discuss the use of active and passive
• transform one to the other.

Writing composition
Children should be able to use the passive voice to 'hide' the perpetrator in a short piece of writing.

Model answers

Pupils' book 4 ▱ A

1 That she is scared of nothing – unflappable!
2 Answers will vary. Perhaps Mrs Sauvage?
3 Perhaps *the ghost of the house.*
4 It means that she couldn't flap and fly – she was literally 'unflappable', as well as being calm and unafraid in her daily life.

Pupils' book 4 ▱ B

5 To hide the name of the murderer.
6 *The wind blew her best hat away. Green slime coated her hands. Something snatched her scarf.*
7 It would make the story less mysterious – and give away who dunnit!

▱ 10A   Who dunnit? ▣

The first, fourth and sixth sentences are active; the rest are passive.
Examples of transformed sentences are: *Butter is stirred in; Satish read the e-mail; Gentlemen will wear top hats; Breakfast is provided; They dissolved the chemicals; The computer was smashed; Samantha passed the football across to Smithy.*

▱ 10B   Who dunnit? ▣

The first, fifth and seventh headlines are active; the rest are passive.
Examples of transformed headlines are: *Cat burglar seized!; Queen discovers burglary; Youth snatches handbag; Aunt Kathryn restored order; Palace beseiged; Terrorists attacked aeroplane; Treasure found in Thames!*

Label each sentence as active or passive. Then transform them.

The cook stirs in the butter.

_____

The e-mail was read.

_____

Top hats will be worn.

_____

We give you breakfast.

_____

The chemicals were dissolved.

_____

Mark smashed the computer.

_____

The football was passed across to Smithy.

_____

Label each newspaper headline as active or passive. Then transform them.

Police seize cat burglar!

_____

Burglary discovered.

_____

Handbag snatched.

_____

Order restored.

_____

Rebels beseige palace.

_____

Aeroplane attacked.

_____

Divers find treasure in Thames!

_____

Active or passive?

Sentences can be written in the active or passive voice. For instance:

The dog bit Ben. (active)

Ben was bitten by the dog. (passive)

In an **active** sentence, the subject (*the dog*) does the action (*bit Ben*). In a **passive** sentence, the subject (*Ben*) is on the receiving end of the action.

The passive allows the 'doer' of the action to be hidden. This means that the passive is useful:

- in some historical texts where it is not known who did what
- in some newspaper reports where the guilty party is so far undetected
- in scientific reports where it doesn't matter who performed certain actions
- in mysteries where it is important to hide 'who dunnit'.

The most common use is probably in everyday speech, especially by young children who want to get out of trouble, e.g.

Mum, the mirror's been broken.

This conveniently disguises who actually broke the mirror, rather than the straight active:

Mum, I broke the mirror.

UNIT 11 Formal language (1)

The purpose of this unit is to identify, understand and use the features of formal language, and consolidate the use of active and passive verbs.

NLS coverage

Key objective

[SL] 1 To investigate further the use of active and passive verbs

[SL] 2 To understand features of formal official language

Learned through:

[TL] **Reading comprehension and writing composition**
17 To read and understand examples of official language and its characteristic features
20 To discuss the way standard English varies in different contexts

[WL] 8 To collect connectives for use in formal writing

Assessment criteria

[SL] By the end of this unit, pupils should be able to identify features of formal language; explain why these conventions exist; begin to use conventions of formal language in their own writing.

[TL] **Writing composition**
Children should be able to produce an example of formal/official writing, e.g. a job advertisement for a ship's cook in Tudor times (link to Primary History Unit 19).

Session 1

You will need OHT 11, PCM 11A and PCM 11B.

Shared reading

1 Begin by explaining to pupils that there are many different types of formal language: in information leaflets, notices, public information documents. In this unit the focus will be on job advertisements.

2 Do pupils know where they might normally find job advertisements? Ask for suggestions. Ensure that pupils cover: local and national newspapers; trade and specialist publications; job centres; shop windows. Discuss the types of advertisement in each setting – e.g. if you wanted someone to deliver newspapers / run an office / be a headteacher.

3 Display, read and discuss OHT 11. Does it sound like a good job? Do they know anyone who would be able to apply? Look at the criteria, salary, etc. Consider the legal position of writers of job adverts. Why must they be accurate?

4 Consider the structure of the advert. Go through it, identifying the type of information included in each section. This will be used later to draw up a frame for an advertisement. Consider the last sentence, and what this means.

5 The advert invites people to ask for more information. What sort of additional information might potential applicants be seeking? Make a list. Discuss whether any of this should have been included in the advert (e.g. closing dates for application).

6 Discuss the layout of the advert. How might it be improved? Discuss implications of altering layout, changing the style and size of some of the type, adding logos – e.g. increased cost but more attractive.

Sentence level work

1 Explain to pupils that during this unit you will be looking at formal, official language. Look again at the advert, and ask them to identify parts that can be described as 'formal'. For example:

- Look for use of pronouns – the owners do not refer to themselves as *we*, but as *the owners* or *Tennessee Jake's*. What effect does this have on the advert? Try reading it with *we*.

- Consider the use of passive forms. Can pupils identify/locate examples of passive constructions? (*Applications are invited...; Further information and an application form may be obtained from:...*). Experiment with changing these into active forms, and discuss the impact. Some might seem clumsy, or long-winded. (*You can apply if you*

are...; If you want to know more and want an application form, contact...)
- Look at use of vocabulary, for example *wish*. What alternatives are there? (Use a thesaurus if necessary.) Is this the best option? Why?

2 Select specific phrases which may be useful in advertisements of this sort, and begin a display – either on OHT, or on a large sheet of sugar paper. Pupils will be able to refer to this collection later.

3 Ask pupils whether the advert is written in standard English. Why is standard English appropriate for adverts of this sort? When might it not be appropriate?

Independent activities

Pupils complete the exercise on PCM 11A. They may use PCM 11B as a writing frame if necessary. Remind them that they can refer to the collection of phrases the class has made.

Plenary

1 Ask pupils which phrases from the collection they used. Were any phrases used more than others? Discuss why this might be.

2 Draw a continuum line:

1	*10*
Informal	*Very formal*

Ask pupils how they would rate Mrs Smith's original request, and the advert they have composed.

Session 2

You will need pupils' book 4, Unit 11, pages 30–31.

Shared reading

1 Explain to pupils that you will be reading two more job adverts. Allow them five minutes to read them, and to decide which job sounds better.

2 Take a quick opinion poll: which job is more attractive? Are there any patterns in who prefers which job (boys/girls, etc.)?

3 Discuss with pupils why they preferred particular jobs, and why they might enjoy them. Look at similarities and differences between the jobs.

4 Trawl through the adverts looking for phrases to add to the display.

Sentence level work

1 Investigate the level of formality of these two advertisements. Use the continuum from the previous session. Look at the way in which the adverts open.

2 Which is more formal, and why? Remind pupils to look for: use of pronouns, passive forms, vocabulary, standard English.

3 Are there any other ways in which these adverts differ? Draw pupils' attention to use of punctuation in the openers:
Angela's Pet Shop: Assistant. £5.50 hourly rate
Saturday Assistant wanted – £33 per day!!

4 Ask pupils to justify their opinions by going through each advert, phrase by phrase.

Independent activities

Children complete questions A and B in the pupils' book. For homework, ask pupils to collect job adverts from a newspaper. Focus on a particular type of job, e.g. teacher / nurse / shop assistant. Pupils sort the adverts into order of formality. They can also look for further phrases for use in writing.

Plenary

Pupils discuss whether it was easier to make phrases more or less formal.

Session 3

You will need pupils' book 4, Unit 11, pages 30–31, and the Reminder Sheet.

Shared writing

Explain to pupils that you will be writing a newspaper advertisement for a job, such as a sailor in Tudor times, maybe on a voyage with Walter Raleigh. Alternatively, you could select a post from other curriculum areas (archaeologist, meteorologist, statistician).

Write together

Using PCM 11B, ask pupils to offer information to be included in each section. Is there any other information that is relevant? Remember that an employer wants the advert to attract the right sort of applicant. Encourage pupils to think of phrases that would be attention-grabbing. Discuss use of standard English. If writing about a historical topic, remind pupils that standard English would have been different in the past.

Independent writing activity

1 Pupils identify a related job (e.g. ship's cook) and plan their advert. If there is time, they may go on to write up the advert as a first draft.

2 Work with a group to challenge them to use the typical phrases identified during the reading sessions, and to include appropriate information. Ask some pupils to write their adverts onto OHT.

Plenary

Share OHT adverts; discuss which ones work best at attracting prospective employees. Do they all have the same level of formality?

Session 4

You will need pupils' book 4, Unit 11, pages 30–31, and the Reminder Sheet.

Shared writing

Take notes / drafted sections from the previous session, and draft/revise them.

Write together

Pupils contribute by suggesting ways collected phrases can be used, experimenting with use of standard English, passive forms, etc. Encourage pupils to manipulate sentences, and try alternative constructions before selecting the most appropriate.

Discuss possibilities for layout. Show how cost varies with space taken up in the newspaper, and increases with use of colour, etc. You could hypothesize about the correlation between space and salary offered!

Independent writing activity

Pupils revise their own advertisements, and present them in layout form. Pick pupils at random to transfer their final adverts onto OHT.

Plenary

Pupils with adverts on OHT share them with the class. Other pupils decide which advert would attract most interest. Remind pupils about legal obligations to give a truthful account of the post offered.

Assessment

Pupils should be able to:
- identify aspects of formal language
- decide which of two or more similar texts is the more formal
- transform sentences from informal to formal, or vice versa, taking account of changes needed
- use elements of formal language in their own writing
- write a job advert, using phrases identified in reading.

Model answers

Pupils' book 4 ◁ A

1 The pet shop job would be ideal – the person would be doing something in which they are interested.
2 Both jobs include a variety of physical tasks.
3 Employers ask for references to make sure that people who apply are suitable, reliable, honest, etc.
4 Literacy and numeracy skills are needed for general duties and when dealing with customers. Angela has asked applicants to write a letter – this can be a good way of checking literacy skills.
5 Answers will vary.

Pupils' book 4 ◁ B

6 Pupils should incorporate aspects of formal and informal language.

◁ 11A   Informal to formal �ⵑ

Comment on the way in which pupils have used the information in the PCM, incorporating the features of formal language. Note whether pupils have been able to use punctuation accurately.

◁ 11B   Writing a job advert ⵑ

Answers will vary.

Mrs Smith telephoned her local newspaper to place an advertisement for a gardener. She wasn't sure exactly how to express what she wanted, so the telephonist said he would write it all down, and ask one of the editors to compose the advert for her. Can you help?

Well, dear, what I really want is a little bit of help with the garden. I'm getting on a bit – not as fit as I once was!

I've been a bit worried about asking, because you don't know who to trust, do you? Do you think I should ask for references? I won't be able to pay that much, only four pounds an hour, and I'll only need a couple of hours a week, I think.

It's not a big garden, but it's got a lawn that needs mowing, and the weeding is back-breaking, really. Mind you, one of my neighbours' boys helped once, and pulled up some of my best plants! I hope that doesn't happen again.

There is a pond, but I've not really kept it up, so it'd be nice if someone knew about ponds and could sort it out for me.

Well, that's it really. I don't want to put my number in – could you ask them to contact the paper and send letters on to me? I think that'd be best. Thank you so much.

Writing a job advert

Use this outline to write an advertisement for a job.

Job title and rate of pay:

Description of job:

Description of person wanted:

How to apply:

Language in **official texts** can be difficult to understand. Various people and organizations have been working hard to make some of these sorts of text easier to read for everyone.

The reasons formal, official texts are difficult to understand are:
The writers often do not talk about themselves. Instead, <u>they name themselves.</u>
For example:
instead of *We want to appoint...* they write *The owners wish to appoint...*

Instead of telling readers what to do, <u>they use passive verbs</u>.
For example:
instead of *You can get application forms from...* they write *Application forms can be obtained from...*

They are very careful about using standard English, so they <u>never contract words</u> (e.g. *don't, couldn't*), and they <u>sometimes use long complex sentences.</u>

Job adverts are often written using formal language. They usually have the same structure. When you are writing an advert for a job, you should include:
- job title and rate of pay
- description of job
- description of person wanted
- how to apply.

Complex sentences (3) – punctuation

The purpose of this unit is to investigate ways of forming and punctuating complex sentences, especially in formal, official writing.

NLS coverage

Key objective

[SL] 3 To revise work on complex sentences:
- ways of connecting clauses
- constructing complex sentences
- appropriate use of punctuation

[SL] 2 To understand features of formal, official language through, e.g.:
- collecting and analysing examples, discussing when and why they are used
- noting the conventions of the language, e.g. use of the impersonal voice, imperative verbs, formal vocabulary
- collecting typical words and expressions

Learned through:

[TL] **Reading comprehension and writing composition**
17 To read and understand examples of official language and its characteristic features, e.g. through discussing consumer information, legal documents, layouts, use of footnotes, instructions, parentheses, headings, appendices and asterisks
20 To discuss the way standard English varies in different contexts, e.g. why legal language is necessarily highly formalized, why questionnaires must be specific

Assessment criteria

[SL] By the end of this unit, pupils should be able to form and punctuate complex sentences; understand and use features of formal language.

[TL] **Writing composition**
Children should be able to write notices using formal style.

Session 1

You will need OHT 12 and PCM 12A.

Shared reading

1 Explain that you will be looking at more examples of formal language, taken from public notices in newspapers which give different types of information. Can pupils think of any examples?

2 The first text is a notice informing readers that a house is available for sale. There is no price quoted; instead, offers are invited from interested people. Ask them to think about why this might be, while they are reading the notice.

3 Display and read OHT 12. Ask pupils what they think about the house: would they like to buy it? Look at phrases that might tell people about what

the house is like. Are there any which would warn <u>against</u> buying a house like this? Consider: *substantial modernization; a comprehensive scheme of refurbishment.*

4 Ask pupils what these phrases mean. Focus first on the adjectives (ask pupils to identify these). What do they mean? What impression do they give?

5 Look at the key nouns – *modernization, refurbishment.* What do they tell us about the house? Consider the implications. Who might have lived in the house previously? We have no direct information about this, but we can infer from the information given.

6 Why would bids have to be sealed?

7 Look at some of the other vocabulary in the notice – for example, the use of the word *tender.* Highlight this as a word which has other meanings – can pupils infer its meaning from the context of the rest of the piece?

Sentence level work

1 Ask pupils to identify elements of formal language from the previous session (use of passive forms, lack of pronouns and contractions, complex sentences).

2 Now look more closely at the complex sentences in the notice. What proportion of sentences are complex?

Sealed bids are invited for informal tender for this property which requires substantial modernization.

The house occupies an elevated position in Valley Road, and would require a comprehensive scheme of refurbishment.

A reception hall, rear lounge, separate dining room, L-shaped kitchen and an enclosed side passage that offers the possibility of being used as a utility room are downstairs.

Upstairs, bedroom one is L-shaped and there are three other bedrooms and a bathroom.

3 It should be clear that a significant proportion of the sentences in the notice are complex; in fact, some are quite difficult to understand (see the third sentence above). Consider ways of making the sentences easier to understand. Work sentence by sentence:

- Sentence 1: underline main clause

  <u>*Sealed bids are invited for informal tender for this property*</u> *which requires substantial modernization.*

  Notice how the second clause expands the noun *property*. This sort of clause, which describes the noun, is called a 'relative clause'. Can pupils find a similar construction in Sentence 3? (*that offers the possibility of being used as a utility room*).

- Sentence 2 – this is a compound sentence with two clauses: 'the house' is the subject of both of them. Ask pupils why the comma is placed where it is. (It marks the boundary between the two clauses.) If the comma were replaced with a full stop, and the *and* with *the house*, there would be two separate sentences.

- Sentence 3 – this is a list with commas between items. Consider the impact of taking out the relative clause. It does not affect the meaning of the sentence – in fact, it makes it a lot easier to understand! Why has the writer put it in? (It tells us about the passage, and makes the house more attractive. It is implying that, although there is no utility room at the moment, one could easily be added.)

- Sentence 4 – again, the writer has tried to put in as much information as possible. Notice how there is a comma after the adverb *upstairs*. Ask pupils to help you rewrite this as a list. For example: *Upstairs there is an L-shaped bedroom, three other bedrooms and a bathroom.* Discuss whether to place a comma after *upstairs*.

Independent activities

Pupils complete PCM 12A. They may work in small groups. You may wish to copy PCM 12A onto OHT for feedback in the plenary.

Plenary

First discuss whether pupils have separated sentences in the same place. Then look at punctuation within sentences – commas, semi-colons, etc. Is there more or less agreement here? Pupils explain why they made the decisions they did.

Session 2

You will need pupils' book 4, Unit 12, pages 32–3, and PCM 12B.

Shared reading

1 Explain to pupils that you will be reading another public notice from a newspaper, this time about roadworks on a main road. You will ask them to give marks out of ten for how easy it is to read and understand.

2 Ask pupils to turn to page 32 in the pupils' book. As this is a difficult text, it is appropriate for you to read it to the pupils.

3 Read the text slowly. Allow pupils some minutes to reread the text on their own, then read it again. Ask pupils if they know what it is about; ask if anyone is willing to try and put it into their own words.

4 Discuss the context in which the notice is published: why is it put in a newspaper? Whereabouts in the newspaper do they think it would be placed? Would anyone read it there? Where else might it be published? How do people normally learn about roadworks? (signs on the road, information on the radio, word of mouth, etc.)

Sentence level work

1 What sorts of mark did pupils give the text for accessibility? Discuss what it is that makes it difficult to read – long sentences, formal and impersonal language.

2 Explain that you are going to be unpicking one of the sentences – the first one. Look at the length of this sentence.

NOTICE IS HEREBY GIVEN that the Engleford Town Council intend not less than seven days from the date hereof to make an order, the effect of which will be to prohibit traffic in either direction along part of the A8040 Tarbin Crossroads to Dengy Rd from its junction with the A88(T) Headly Rd in a southerly direction to its junction with the Class III road at Dengy.

3 Work to make the sentence more accessible by reducing the information in it:

NOTICE IS HEREBY GIVEN that the Engleford Town Council intend ~~not less than seven days from the date hereof~~ to make an order, ~~the effect of which will be~~ to prohibit traffic in either direction along part of the A8040 Tarbin Crossroads to Dengy Rd from its junction with the A88(T) Headly Rd in a southerly direction to its junction with the Class III road at Dengy.

4 Look at other ways of making the sentence easier to read, for example making the language more active:

In seven days, Engleford Town Council are going to prohibit traffic in either direction along part of the A8040 from its junction with the A88(T) Headly Rd, south to its junction with the road at Dengy.

5 There are other phrases which could be changed – for example, *prohibit traffic in either direction*. Can pupils think of alternatives? Look at what this does to the sentence as a whole.

6 Consider changes in punctuation that are necessary. For example, the adverbial phrase *In seven days* can be followed by a comma. How does this help? Try reading this sentence with and without the comma. Discuss whether the original sentence could have been made easier to read with punctuation. Punctuate the sentence with pupils, for example:

NOTICE IS HEREBY GIVEN that the Engleford Town Council intend (not less than seven days from the date hereof) to make an order, the effect of which will be to prohibit traffic – in either direction – along part of the A8040 Tarbin Crossroads to Dengy Rd (from its junction with the A88(T) Headly Rd in a southerly direction to its junction with the Class III road at Dengy).

7 Does this help? Share pupils' perceptions, and look at alternatives.

Independent activities

Children complete questions A and B in the pupils' book. Use PCM 12B as an extension or homework activity. This asks pupils to match formal sentences with their less formal counterparts.

Plenary

Discuss how pupils carried out this task. Which were the easiest to do? Which sentences do pupils prefer – the formal or the informal? Which are complex sentences?

Session 3

You will need pupils' book 4, Unit 12, pages 32–3, and the Reminder Sheet.

Shared writing

Explain to pupils that you will be writing a notice for the school. Discuss possible topics, e.g. notice to parents about arrangements for holidays / school clubs – even dates of SATs week! You will be doing two versions of the same information – one as accessible as possible, one as formal as possible, and ask for parents', teachers' and pupils' views.

Write together

Begin with the less formal version of the notice. Decide the order in which information is to be presented, and draft it. Discuss, as you are working, what level of informality is appropriate. For example, should contracted forms (*won't, shouldn't*, etc.) be used? How long should sentences be? Complex sentences will be useful, because they are necessary when giving reasons for changes in routine and so on. Discuss, as you write, alternatives for punctuating these sentences. Explain that punctuation often marks grammatical boundaries. Within sentences, there is often some degree of personal preference as to how punctuation is used.

Independent writing activity

Pupils write their own versions of the notice. You may wish to offer some pupils alternative notices to write – more or less challenging. For homework, ask pupils to collect phrases from formal notices in newspapers that they can use in their own work.

Plenary

Pupils report back on their work. Ask each one to explain a key decision they made, and talk about a complex sentence they have composed.

Session 4

You will need pupils' book 4, Unit 12, pages 32–3, and the Reminder Sheet.

Shared writing

Display the version of the notice written during the previous session. Remind pupils that they will be writing a more formal version which gives the same information. This session should be fun – they should work on making the notice as formal as possible. Remind them how difficult the beginning of the pupils' book text was: can they aim for something similar?

Write together

Using phrases pupils have found in notices they have read, rewrite the notice as formally as possible. Aim for very complex sentences. Discuss use of punctuation as you write.

Independent writing activity

Pupils compose the formal version of their own notice, using similar devices and vocabulary to that they have experienced. Work with a group who may find this difficult, focusing on sentence construction and punctuation.

Plenary

Pupils read their notices aloud. Others have to give marks out of ten to each. The aim is to produce something formal but still understandable – even if only just!

Assessment

Pupils should be able to:
• use the vocabulary and language forms of formal writing
• compose and punctuate complex sentences.
Comment on the extent to which pupils have captured the tone of 'officialese'.
Discuss with pupils how accessible their notices are, and which one should be published where.

Model answers

Pupils' book 4 ☐ **A**

1 They are building a new road.
2 Answers will vary. Pupils should refer to the maximum stated, the possibility of delays, etc.
3 Answers will vary. Pupils may feel that some drivers will complain; others will be glad that there will be a better road at the end of it.
4 So that local people can find out about it, and tell each other.
5 By word of mouth, from notices on the road, internet, RAC and AA, radio announcements.

Pupils' book 4 ☐ **B**

6 Answers will vary.

☐**12A** Complex sentences (3) – punctuation ▯
Answers may vary; this is a guide:
A well-appointed property in a popular area of Grimsham is being offered at £63,000. The semi-detached house in Oakford Avenue has been well maintained and is well worth an inspection. // On the ground floor, a hall leads to the lounge (16' x 15') having double-glazed leaded windows and traditional-style fireplace with marble hearth. A dining area (8' x 8') has a double-glazed patio door giving access to the rear garden. The kitchen includes a built-in four-ring gas hob and electric oven. There is a separate morning room. // Upstairs there are three bedrooms and a bathroom. // To the front of the property is a lawn, and to the rear a flagged patio with flower beds and borders.
Roberts and Weeks: 03692 119988

☐**12B** Sentence matching ▯

Right of admission reserved.	We might not let you in.
Vehicles left at owners' risk.	If your car is stolen, it's not our fault.
Sealed bids are invited for tender for this property.	You can put in a bid for this house if you wish.
No ball games allowed.	You can't play soccer here.
Application forms can be obtained from Miller's.	You can get an application form from Miller's.
Stubborn stains may require a second application.	You might have to do this again.
One month's notice required in the event of cancellation.	You have to tell us a month before if you want to cancel.

This notice has not been edited, and there is no punctuation. Read it through once, then go through it and mark sentences with a full stop and capital letter, and paragraphs with //. Next, look at the sentences and decide what other punctuation is needed. Make any further improvements you would like.

a well-appointed property in a popular area of grimsham is being offered at £63000 the semi detached house in oakford avenue has been well maintained and is well worth an inspection on the ground floor a hall leads to the lounge 16' x 15' having double glazed leaded windows and traditional style fireplace with marble hearth a dining area 8' x 8' has a double glazed patio door giving access to the rear garden the kitchen includes a built in four ring gas hob and electric oven there is a separate morning room upstairs there are three bedrooms and a bathroom to the front of the property is a lawn and to the rear a flagged patio with flower beds and borders.

roberts and weeks 03692 119988

Here are some sentences which are written in a very formal style. The second set is less formal. Can you match them up?

Right of admission reserved.	You can put in a bid for this house if you wish.
Vehicles left at owners' risk.	You can get an application form from Miller's.
Sealed bids are invited for tender for this property.	You might have to do this again.
No ball games allowed.	You have to tell us a month before if you want to cancel.
Application forms can be obtained from Miller's.	You can't play soccer here.
Stubborn stains may require a second application.	We might not let you in.
One month's notice required in the event of cancellation.	If your car is stolen, it's not our fault.

Which sentences were easiest to match? Explain why.

Punctuation is used to help readers understand what writers mean. Punctuation is particularly important in complex sentences. Sometimes, writers make sentences so complex that they are hard to understand.

Look at the following extract from a notice:

> NOTICE IS HEREBY GIVEN that the Engleford Town Council intend not less than seven days from the date hereof to make an order, the effect of which will be to prohibit traffic in either direction along part of the A8040 Tarbin Crossroads to Dengy Rd from its junction with the A88(T) Headly Rd in a southerly direction to its junction with the Class III road at Dengy.

This has been made easier by taking out or changing words:

> In seven days, Engleford Town Council are going to prohibit traffic in either direction along part of the A8040 from its junction with the A88(T) Headly Rd, south to its junction with the road at Dengy.

It can also be made easier to read by adding punctuation:

> NOTICE IS HEREBY GIVEN that the Engleford Town Council intend (not less than seven days from the date hereof) to make an order, the effect of which will be to prohibit traffic – in either direction – along part of the A8040 Tarbin Crossroads to Dengy Rd (from its junction with the A88(T) Headly Rd in a southerly direction to its junction with the Class III road at Dengy).

UNIT 13 — Complex sentences (4) – variation

The purpose of this unit is to investigate ways of varying sentences. This will allow pupils to extend the range of sentence structures they use, considering the needs of the reader.

NLS coverage

Key objective

SL 3 To revise work on complex sentences: identifying main clauses; ways of connecting clauses; constructing complex sentences

Learned through:

TL Reading comprehension and writing composition
2 To analyse how individual paragraphs are structured in writing, e.g. comments sequenced to follow the shifting thoughts of a character
7 To identify the key features of different types of literary text
13 To parody a literary text, describing stock characters and plot structure, language, etc.

Assessment criteria

SL By the end of this unit, pupils should be able to:
- identify and use different types of sentence opening
- vary the structure of complex sentences, using connectives

TL Writing composition
Children should be able to write in the style of an author, using typical structures and language.

Session 1

You will need OHT 13 and PCMs 13A and 13B.

Shared reading

1 Explain to pupils that you will be reading an extract from a mystery story. Do pupils know of any famous mystery writers? Or literary detectives?

2 Cover all of OHT 13 except for the first sentence. Read the first sentence to the class. Can pupils say whether or not the writing is set in modern times?

3 Read the rest of the text aloud. Have pupils revised their view? If so, what clues were there? Draw their attention to the reference to *Dr Watson*. Does this trigger any memories?

4 Pupils may remember Sherlock Holmes. If not, introduce the name, and ask if pupils know anything about him, or about his famous cases.

5 Explain that you will be reading another extract from the beginning of this story, *The Red-Headed League*, in the next sessions. Pupils should think about how the writer, Arthur Conan Doyle, writes. What makes his writing different from, say, Charles Dickens, Roald Dahl or Jacqueline Wilson?

6 Draw pupils' attention to the fact that this entire extract represents part of one utterance. How can they know this? They should be able to identify the speech marks and the use of ellipsis at the beginning of the text. The fact that the ellipses are within the speech marks indicates that the character has previously been saying something.

7 Ask pupils to summarize what Holmes is saying – basically, he doesn't have the answer. He is puzzled!

8 Look at the range of words Holmes uses for *unusual* – including *singular, peculiar, unique*. Plot the sequence of his thinking, and unpick it to make sure that pupils understand the language. Ask them whether they found it easy to read.

Sentence level work

1 Discuss Conan Doyle's sentences: would pupils say they were complex? How complex, on a scale of 1 – 5? Explain that you will be looking at the sentences to see how complex they are.

2 *As far as I have heard it is impossible for me to say whether the present case is an instance of crime or not, but the course of events is certainly among the most singular that I have ever listened to.*

82

Look at this sentence. Can pupils work out how many clauses there are? (There are two.) How can they identify the boundary between the clauses? There is a natural break here, where the sentence could be broken down into two shorter sentences. In addition, there are a comma and a conjunction which draw attention to the boundary.

3 Try using this sentence to write about something else, e.g. a disputed goal in football. Help children to use the structure and vocabulary to create the sort of sentence he might have used.
   As far as I have seen it is impossible for me to say whether that was a goal or not, but the move was certainly among the most exciting that I have ever seen.

Independent activities

Pupils complete PCM 13A or 13B. Most pupils should be able to complete 13A, which will help with 13B. Some may be able to start with 13B.

Plenary

Discuss the challenges pupils faced using Holmes' style for a football commentary.

Session 2

You will need pupils' book 4, Unit 13, pages 34–5.

Shared reading

1 Explain that the pupils' book text follows on from the extract on OHT. Watson describes Mr Wilson as an average person, but Holmes is able to work out a lot about him from his appearance.

2 Allow pupils five minutes to read the text to themselves. Then ask them to work in pairs to rehearse the brief exchange between Holmes and Wilson, focusing on their feelings about each other.

3 Invite pairs to read out their interpretations of the exchange, and explain what decisions they made about how to play the parts. Is there much agreement? How do pupils think Dr Watson felt?

Sentence level work

1 Remind pupils that you have been looking at different sentence structures, and that you will be investigating types of sentence in this text. Ask them to scan for any sentence types they recognize.

2 Pupils may identify lists, for example:
   Our visitor bore every mark of being …
   He wore rather baggy grey shepherd's check trousers, …
   Beyond the obvious facts that he has at some time …

3 Classify the types of list. Look at the items: are they adjectives or phrases? Discuss the punctuation.

4 Ask pupils why there are so many lists at this part of the story. Link description and lists.

5 Ask pupils to look for other sentence types, for example, complex sentences:
   As he glanced down the advertisement column, with his head thrust forward …
   I took a good look at the man and endeavoured, after the fashion of my companion, to read the indications which might be presented by his dress or appearance.

6 For each of these examples, challenge pupils to identify the main ideas (underlined above). What is essential in the sentence? What is it that the sentence is about? Rewrite each sentence as one clause.

7 Discuss the way Conan Doyle has varied sentence types. Are his sentences generally short or long? Is there much variety? What effect does this have?

Independent activities

Children complete questions A and B in the pupils' book. One group of questions may be set as homework.

Plenary

Review pupils' responses to the text. What did they find as they completed the activity? How will they go about completing the remaining activity?

Session 3

You will need pupils' book 4, Unit 13, pages 34–5, and the Reminder Sheet.

Shared writing

1 Explain to pupils that you will be writing a parody of the text. Explain that this is when one writer uses what they know of the work of another writer to compose a piece which is similar. The writer wants readers to know that they are pretending to write like the original. It is a sort of literary joke.

2 Make a list of the things pupils know about Conan Doyle from what they have read. Remind them about the use of lists, complex sentences, variation in sentence structures.

3 Now plan a similar scenario:
   Characters: one expert and his/her friend;
   a stranger, asking help from the expert.
   Setting: suggest a modern setting – this will be less confusing. Ask pupils to think up their own ideas as the class carries on writing.

Write together

Write a paragraph plan based on the extracts from *The Red-Headed League*. Look at the content of each paragraph, and list what should be included.

Independent writing activity

Pupils begin to write, using their own characters and ideas. Remind them to refer to the paragraph plan and the Reminder Sheet.

Plenary

1 Share pupils' ideas and initial thoughts – are there any paragraphs with which pupils are particularly happy? Look at the sentence structures used.
2 Select one draft for use in the next session: check this with the pupil who wrote it.

Session 4

You will need pupils' book 4, Unit 13, pages 34–5, and the Reminder Sheet.

Shared writing

Take the draft from the previous session. Read it together. Look back at the original work, and identify features which match.

Write together

Identify points at which the writing does not 'ring true'. Revise the work, importing features from Conan Doyle's writing. Focus on sentence structure and variation, as well as the tone of the writing.

Independent writing activity

Pupils complete and revise their writing.

Plenary

Ask pupils to share their strategies for parodying the writing. What was easy, what was difficult? Did they find any features easier to use than others? Why?

Assessment

Pupils should be able to:
• identify complex sentences
• locate the main idea / main clause in a sentence
• compose complex sentences
• identify characteristic features of the writing of Conan Doyle
• write in the style of Conan Doyle.

Model answers

Pupils' book 4 ☐ **A**

1 He says Wilson was *'average'*, *'obese, pompous and slow'*. This suggests Watson does not like him.
2 Watson describes Wilson's clothes as shabby and faded, so we assume that he is not very well off.
3 Answers will vary; he was probably amazed, maybe embarrassed. Pupils should justify their answers.
4 Answers will vary; he may have been surprised.
5 He has probably come to ask for help with finding something out. He has brought a newspaper – it might be something to do with that.

Pupils' book 4 ☐ **B**

6 Answers will vary.
7 Answers will vary.
8 *and; as; however; altogether; beyond*

☐**13A   Complex to simple** 🄿

Perhaps, Mr. Wilson…	Could you start again?
I ask you not merely…	Dr. Watson would like…
In the present instance I am forced to admit…	I have never heard of anything like this at all.
Now, Mr. Jabez Wilson here…	This is going to be a really good story.
As a rule, when I have heard…	I can usually remember something similar.

☐**13B   Writing complex sentences** 🄿
Answers will vary.

These complex sentences from the text have been simplified. Can you match them up?

Perhaps, Mr. Wilson, you would have the great kindness to recommence your narrative.	Dr. Watson would like to hear the beginning and I would like to hear it again.
I ask you not merely because my friend Dr. Watson has not heard the opening part but also because the peculiar nature of the story makes me anxious to have every possible detail from your lips.	This is going to be a really good story.
In the present instance I am forced to admit that the facts are, to the best of my belief, unique.	I can usually remember something similar.
Now, Mr. Jabez Wilson here has been good enough to call upon me this morning, and to begin a narrative which promises to be one of the most singular which I have listened to for some time.	I have never heard of anything like this at all.
As a rule, when I have heard some slight indication of the course of events, I am able to guide myself by the thousands of other similar cases which occur to my memory.	Could you start again?

Sentences from *The Red-Headed League* by Arthur Conan Doyle

Sherlock Holmes has started commentating on football. Use these sentences as models to write new sentences about a football match.

> Perhaps, Mr. Wilson, you would have the great kindness to recommence your narrative.

> As a rule, when I have heard some slight indication of the course of events, I am able to guide myself by the thousands of other similar cases which occur to my memory.

> I ask you not merely because my friend Dr. Watson has not heard the opening part but also because the peculiar nature of the story makes me anxious to have every possible detail from your lips.

> In the present instance I am forced to admit that the facts are, to the best of my belief, unique.

Sentences from *The Red-Headed League* by Arthur Conan Doyle

13 Complex sentences (4) – variation

Many writers use complex sentences because they help to link ideas and are easier for readers to follow than lots of short sentences.

There are different types of complex sentence, and writers often have their own favourite types. In the extracts you have read, Arthur Conan Doyle uses many sentences which contain lists:

> Our visitor bore every mark of being an average commonplace British tradesman, obese, pompous, and slow.
>
> Beyond the obvious facts that he has at some time done manual labour, that he takes snuff, that he is a Freemason, that he has been in China, and that he has done a considerable amount of writing lately, I can deduce nothing else.

Conan Doyle often writes complex sentences with connectives at the beginning:

> Altogether, look as I would, there was nothing remarkable about the man save his blazing red head, and the expression of extreme chagrin and discontent upon his features.
>
> As he glanced down the advertisement column, with his head thrust forward and the paper flattened out upon his knee, …

Sentences from *The Red-Headed League* by Arthur Conan Doyle

Contracting sentences

The purpose of this unit is to investigate ways of contracting sentences and building notes back up into connected prose.

NLS coverage

Key objective

[SL] 4 To revise work on contracting sentences: summary; note making; editing

Learned through:

[TL] **Reading comprehension and writing composition**
1 To understand aspects of narrative structure, e.g. how chapters in a book (or paragraphs in a short story or chapter) are linked together; how authors handle time
8, 9 To analyse the success of texts and writers in evoking particular responses in the reader; to increase familiarity with significant writers of the past
12 To study one genre and produce an extended piece of similar writing

Assessment criteria

[SL] By the end of this unit, pupils should be able to: identify main ideas in sentences; contract sentences, retaining main ideas; expand note-forms into longer sentences.

[TL] **Writing composition**
Children should be able to write in the style of an author, using typical structures and language.

Session 1

You will need OHT 14 and PCM 14A.

Shared reading

1 Explain to pupils that you will be reading an extract from a book written almost 100 years ago. It is from *The War of the Worlds* by H.G. Wells. Discuss with pupils what the book might be about.

2 Display and read OHT 14. Ask pupils to revise their ideas about the story in the book.

3 Discuss the text itself. What is the main emotion the narrator is feeling? Is the writing convincing – does it make pupils feel a bit like the narrator?

4 Move on to look at one of the ways in which the writer conveys fear and panic. How long does this part of the story last? As long as it takes to read it? Longer? Shorter? Reread the text with the pupils. Do different paragraphs seem to move at different paces? Look at how Wells does this.

Sentence level work

1 Explain that you will be looking at contracting sentences; first into shorter sentences, then into notes. From earlier work on this, can pupils predict which words will need to be retained for short sentences? Probably nouns, verbs and prepositions.

2 Now look at a sentence from the first paragraph:
For a moment perhaps I stood there, breast-high in the almost boiling water, dumbfounded at my position, hopeless of escape.
This can be contracted to:
For a moment I stood in the water, hopeless.
Discuss whether or not the opening adverbial – *For a moment* – is essential.
It may be that if writing this as a short sentence, words would be re-sequenced. For example:
I stood in the water for a moment, hopeless.
Hopeless, I stood in the water for a moment.
The sentence could be reduced even further:
I stood in the water.
How could this be transformed into a note?
Stood in water.

3 If these three words represent the 'bare bones' of the sentence, then the other words must tell us something about how Wells created the sense of fear. Discuss which words achieve this effect, and how changing the order can change it.

4 Now look at a sentence from the third paragraph, and take it through the same process.

5 Wells has used some very short sentences in this passage. Why? Look at them. (Pupils should notice that they are often at the end of paragraphs.)

Independent activities

1 Distribute PCM 14A. This extract is from earlier in the book, and describes the narrator's first sight of the Martians. Remind pupils that this is description, not narrative. Will the same kinds of word be deleted? Pupils should practise deleting words until they have short sentences, then rewrite the text in note form, almost like a police report.

2 Work with one or two groups, supporting pupils identifying main ideas and transforming shorter sentences into notes.

Plenary

Invite pupils to read their notes aloud, as if presenting a description in court. Discuss what was necessary to include. Which words were essential? Were there any difficult words in the passage? Ask pupils to explain how they worked out the meanings of these.

Session 2

You will need pupils' book 4, Unit 14, pages 36–7, and PCM 14B.

Shared reading

1 Remind pupils that in the previous session they looked at an extract in which things happened very quickly.

2 Ask pupils to turn to page 36 in the pupils' book. Allow them five minutes to read the passage through a couple of times. As they are reading, they should be considering what length of time the passage covers. How does the passage make them feel? How much detail is there? What do they think the narrator is doing during this time?

3 Now read the text to the pupils.

4 How does Wells make it seem as if time is passing very slowly? Look at the way he repeats sentence openings, and uses phrases such as *during this time*.

5 Briefly discuss Wells' style. Pupils have read three passages from *The War of the Worlds*. Can they make any generalizations about the way in which he writes? Do they think they would like to read the whole book? Ask them to explain their answers.

Sentence level work

1 In the previous session, the text was put into note form in two stages. In this session, it will be done straight away, without deletions.

2 Reread the passage and ask pupils to identify the main idea in the first paragraph. Paraphrase and reduce it to note form, for example:
– Day 12: throat painful. Drank water from pump. Noise did not disturb Martians.
The sentences are much shorter in this version. Discuss whether all the essential information is included. Look at alternative notes based on this paragraph; try a range of possible versions. Remind pupils that there is no 'right' answer.

Independent activities

Children complete questions A and B in the pupils' book. Use PCM 14B as an alternative to question 7 for pupils who would be able to tackle an unfamiliar text.

Plenary

Discuss the purposes of note-taking. In information texts, it helps us record information we wish to remember. In narrative, it helps us to uncover the plot structure and summarize the story.

Session 3

You will need pupils' book 4, Unit 14, pages 36–7, and the Reminder Sheet.

Shared writing

Explain that you will be writing a story about a battle and its aftermath. Discuss the way in which Wells used time in the extracts from *The War of the Worlds*. Offer pupils an adapted plot structure, and discuss what should be included in each section. For example:

Creatures emerge	Set the scene; realization Description of creatures
Destroy all in sight	Action-packed, fast-moving. How does character escape?
Main character goes into hiding	Slower, description of problems and how they worsen
Realizes after time that creatures no longer there	Excitement
Emerges to find others still alive	Feelings of joy; reunions with family / friends
Rebuilds civilization	Beginning only – links to future

Write together

1 Draw attention to the way you have used notes or contracted sentences to describe the plot and flesh out the content. What advantages does this have?

2 Explain that the story pupils write will follow this structure; each section will be of a similar length.

3 Develop the first section. Make further notes on the progress of the plot, using pupils' contributions and recording in note form onto OHT/flipchart/board so that pupils can refer to it later.

Independent writing activity

Pupils write up their own first sections. Make sure they know that they can use either their own or the shared ideas.

Plenary

Consider the second section. Reminding pupils to use note form, ask them to jot down two ideas onto whiteboard/scrap paper and feedback to class. Build up an outline for the second section from this. Pupils may continue working on the story for homework.

Session 4

You will need pupils' book 4, Unit 14, pages 36–7, and the Reminder Sheet.

Shared writing

Review one version of the second section from the story. This may be a pupil's work, or a draft of your own. Remind pupils that things happen very quickly during this part of the story, and this needs to be reflected in the language. Revisit Wells' version from the OHT and use some of his sentence structures, vocabulary, etc. to improve the pace of the writing.

Write together

Move on to the next section, in which there are few events. How can you cover the way time passes slowly?

Independent writing activity

Pupils continue writing, revising their second section, and moving on to complete the story. Work with groups to ensure that there are changes of pace in their stories. Share ideas and take constructive feedback.

Plenary

Pupils discuss how they tried to vary the pace of their writing, and give examples of what they have done. It may be useful to begin with some examples from the group(s) with which you have been working.

Assessment

Pupils should be able to:
- shorten sentences by deleting words which are not necessary
- write in note form, e.g. when planning
- build notes back up into connected prose
- vary the pace of their writing to reflect the plot.

Model answers

Pupils' book 4 ☐ A

1 He is hiding from the Martians – he thinks they will kill him.

2 Pupils may refer to fear of the unknown, thirst and hunger, isolation.

3 The narrator may have been relieved to hear a familiar sound.

4 He mentions that the dog could give him away, and he could eat the dog.

5 Answers will vary.

Pupils' book 4 ☐ A

6 and 7 Answers will vary.

☐ 14A Contracting sentences ⏸

Answers will vary; this is a rough guide:
Two eyes were regarding me. The head was rounded, and had a face with a mouth and eyes. It heaved and pulsated. A lank tentacle gripped the edge of the cylinder, another swayed in the air. The horror of its appearance: V-shaped mouth, pointed upper lip, no brow ridges, no chin, mouth quivering, Gorgon tentacles, tumultuous breathing, heaviness and painfulness of movement – the immense eyes. Oily brown skin, clumsy movements. I was overcome with disgust and dread.

☐ 14B Contracting sentences ⏸

Make sure pupils include all essential details.

14A Contracting sentences

Look at the text below, which is a description from *The War of the Worlds*.
Read it through twice. Then take out words that are not essential to
meaning. Remember that this is a description. When you feel you have just
the 'bare bones', rewrite the text in note form.

When you have finished, look back and see which sorts of word were
essential.

Martian description

Two large dark-coloured eyes were
regarding me steadfastly. The mass
that framed them, the head of the
thing, was rounded, and had, one might
say, a face. There was a mouth under the
eyes, the lipless brim of which quivered and panted, and
dropped saliva. The whole creature heaved and pulsated
convulsively. A lank tentacular appendage gripped the edge of
the cylinder, another swayed in the air.

Those who have never seen a living Martian can scarcely
imagine the strange horror of its appearance. The peculiar V-
shaped mouth with its pointed upper lip, the absence of brow
ridges, the absence of a chin beneath the wedgelike lower lip,
the incessant quivering of this mouth, the Gorgon groups of
tentacles, the tumultuous breathing of the lungs in a strange
atmosphere, the evident heaviness and painfulness of movement
due to the greater gravitational energy of the earth – above all,
the extraordinary intensity of the immense eyes – were at once
vital, intense, inhuman, crippled and monstrous. There was
something fungoid in the oily brown skin, something in the
clumsy deliberation of the tedious movements unspeakably
nasty. Even at this first encounter, this first glimpse, I was
overcome with disgust and dread.

From *The War of the Worlds* by H.G. Wells (William Heinemann, 1898), reprinted by
permission of A.P. Watt Ltd on behalf of the Executors of the Estate of H.G. Wells.

Contracting sentences

Rewrite this extract in note form. Remember to include only essential detail.

Death by fire

I stood staring, not as yet realising that this was death leaping from man to man in that little distant crowd. All I felt was that it was something very strange. An almost noiseless and blinding flash of light, and a man fell headlong and lay still; and as the unseen shaft of heat passed over them, pine trees burst into fire, and every dry furze bush became with one dull thud a mass of flames. And far away towards Knaphill I saw the flashes of trees and hedges and wooden buildings suddenly set alight.

It was sweeping round swiftly and steadily, this flaming death, this invisible, inevitable sword of heat. I perceived it coming towards me by the flashing bushes it touched, and was too astounded and stupefied to stir. I heard the crackle of fire in the sand pits and the sudden squeal of a horse that was as suddenly stilled. Then it was as if an invisible yet intensely heated finger were drawn through the heather between me and the Martians, and all along a curving line beyond the sand pits the dark ground smoked and crackled. Something fell with a crash far away to the left where the road from Woking station opens out on the common. Forthwith the hissing and humming ceased, and the black, dome-like object sank slowly out of sight into the pit.

All this had happened with such swiftness that I had stood motionless, dumbfounded and dazzled by the flashes of light. Had that death swept through a full circle, it must inevitably have slain me in my surprise. But it passed and spared me, and left the night about me suddenly dark and unfamiliar.

From *The War of the Worlds* by H.G. Wells (William Heinemann, 1898), reprinted by permission of A.P. Watt Ltd on behalf of the Executors of the Estate of H.G. Wells.

14 Contracting sentences

Shorter sentences

There are many times when it is not necessary to write in full sentences, for example: when leaving a note for a friend or family member, when recording useful information from a programme or a book, or when planning.

When **taking notes** from something you have read, make sure that you include the main points. One way of doing this is to cross out words that are not necessary, for example:

I screamed ~~aloud~~, and ~~scalded, half blinded, agonised, I~~ staggered ~~through the leaping, hissing water~~ towards the shore.

I screamed and staggered towards the shore.

In note form, this might read:

Screamed, staggered towards shore.

You can also **use notes to plan**. When you are writing a story, it is useful to know how long each section will be, and what you are going to include in it. For example:

Creatures emerge
Destroy all in sight
Main character goes into hiding
Realizes after a period that creatures no longer there
Emerges to find others still alive
Rebuilds civilization

Conditionals

The purpose of this unit is to introduce and develop the use of conditional forms, particularly in the writing of discussion texts. This will allow pupils to develop more complex arguments.

NLS coverage

Key objective

SL 5 To use reading to:
- investigate conditionals, e.g. *if ... then, might, could, would*
- use these forms to construct sentences which express, e.g. possibilities, hypotheses
- explore use of conditionals in past and future

Learned through:

TL Reading comprehension and writing composition
2 To analyse how individual paragraphs are structured in writing
16 To identify the features of balanced written arguments
14 To write commentaries or summaries crediting views expressed
19 To write a balanced report of a controversial issue: summarizing fairly the competing views; analysing strengths and weaknesses of different positions
WL **8** To build a bank of useful terms and phrases for argument

Assessment criteria

SL By the end of this unit, pupils should be able to identify different types of conditional; vary openings for different purposes.

TL Writing composition
Children should be able to write a persuasive text, using conditionals appropriately.

Session 1

You will need OHT 15 and PCM 15A.

Shared reading

1 Ask pupils to discuss how they go about making choices and decisions. Have they been involved in any major or day-to-day decisions recently? Do they always get their own way? Do they ever change their minds? Discuss the way in which some decisions are made on their own (which sweets/books to buy), while some involve others. If they disagreed with someone else involved, what strategies could they use to persuade them?

2 Explain that you will be sharing a text which is about decisions. It shows something people often do to make a decision: a list of pros and cons. This means points for and against a particular course of action.

3 Display and read OHT 15 to pupils. Discuss which reasons pupils feel are most persuasive, on both sides. Are there any other points that have not been made?

4 Ask children which fire they would choose. Discuss the reasons. How much was their decision based on the evidence and reasons presented in the text, and how much on their own experience, or images of fires they have seen / read about, etc.?

Sentence level work

1 Explain that you are going to look at a particular sort of clause – conditional. What do pupils understand by the term 'condition'? It has more than one meaning. Discuss alternative meanings, and then explain the grammatical meaning. This is a sort of sentence in which the speaker or writer explains that if one thing happens, then there may be certain consequences. Experiment with making sentences with conditional clauses from the information on the OHT. Demonstrate the first one: *If you have a coal fire, you have to clean it regularly.*

2 Ask pupils to generate three or four other sentences which follow a similar pattern. Ensure pupils understand where the comma occurs in these sentences. Ask pupils to identify the key word which occurs in all of these sentences: *if.*

3 Now demonstrate altering the sequence of clauses in this sentence, for example:
You have to do a lot of cleaning if you have a coal fire.

4 Discuss the differences between the two sentences, in terms of impact, order and punctuation.

5 Distribute whiteboards/paper. Challenge pupils to alter their other sentences in the same way. Discuss the changes they have made.

Independent activities

Pupils complete PCM 15A. This asks them to practise writing sentences with conditional clauses.

Plenary

Share pupils' responses to this activity. Begin by selecting one point, and ask three or four pupils to give their responses. Discuss these responses and ask pupils to select the most effective sentence, and explain why.

Session 2

You will need pupils' book 4, Unit 15, pages 38–9, and PCM 15B.

Shared reading

1 Explain to pupils that you will be looking at a discussion text which relates to a health issue. Ask pupils if they clean their teeth every day (hope for a 100% response on this one!). Can pupils name any of the ingredients in toothpaste? Offer fluoride and ask if anyone knows what it does.

2 Ask pupils to turn to page 38 of the pupils' book. Where has this text come from? Pupils should notice that it is a question and answer. It could have come from a website, a magazine or newspaper.

3 Read the question together, and discuss briefly.

4 Now, ask pupils to read the first paragraph of the answer on their own. What impression do they get? Note the strong first sentence in support of fluoride.

5 Go on to read the rest of the text together.

6 Discuss pupils' feelings about fluoride. Do they have the same feelings after reading the whole text as they had after reading the first paragraph? If not, how have their feelings changed?

Sentence level work

1 Ask pupils if they noticed any conditional clauses in the text. Go through the text, asking pupils to read aloud the conditional clauses. Practise changing the order of clauses within the sentences, orally. For example:
Almost all medicines can have an adverse effect – or even be deadly – if they are not taken as directed.
If they are not taken as directed, most medicines can have an adverse effect.

2 Both of these sentences contain the word *if*. Consider other possibilities, for example *unless* or *as long as*.
Most medicines can have an adverse effect, unless they are taken as directed.
Most medicines do not have an adverse effect, as long as you take them as directed.

3 Discuss the difference in emphasis between these two sentences.

4 Follow the same procedure with one of the other sentences containing a conditional clause.

Independent activities

Children complete questions A and B in the pupils' book. They fill in PCM 15B for use in the plenary.

Plenary

Discuss pupils' responses. In preparation for Session 3, build up a class list of points in favour of travelling by car and by train.

Session 3

You will need pupils' book 4, Unit 15, pages 38–9, and the Reminder Sheet.

Shared writing

1 Explain to pupils that you will be writing up a discussion, e.g. whether a family should travel by car or by train. Review advantages and disadvantages of each mode of travel, referring back to the class list built up in the previous session. Add further ideas or suggestions to the list.

2 Discuss the structure of the written discussion. Should all points be included? In which order should points be tackled, e.g. most important issues first?

Write together

1 On OHT, map out a page. Identify space allocated for the opening statement, paragraphs relating to

specific issues, and a conclusion. Discuss space allocation for body text as opposed to opening and closing paragraphs: should they be of equal length?

2 Revise grammatical features of discussion texts. Focus on the use of conditionals.

Independent writing activity

Assign pupils to different sides of the discussion. Explain that their work will be marked for persuasiveness. Pupils begin writing.

Plenary

Review the grammatical features of conditional sentences, from the Reminder Sheet. Invite pupils to share examples from their own writing. Copy one piece onto OHT for revision in the next session.

Session 4

You will need pupils' book 4, Unit 15, pages 38–9, a piece of pupil's work copied onto OHT, and the Reminder Sheet.

Shared writing

1 Display the selected piece of work. Allow pupils time to read it to themselves, then read it aloud. Ask pupils to identify three good things about the text. Highlight these in green. Discuss why they have been selected.

2 Now ask pupils to identify two places in which the piece can be improved. Discuss and agree as a class. Highlight these sentences/phrases in orange.

Write together
Work together on these sections of text. Check the use of conditional forms, and experiment with these.

Independent writing activity

Pupils continue to work on their own writing.

Plenary

Pupils share what they still need to do to complete their work. Set targets for completion; remind pupils that they will be marked for persuasiveness.

Assessment

Pupils should be able to:
• identify and manipulate conditional forms
• use conditional forms accurately and appropriately in their own writing
• write a discussion piece using conditional forms.

Model answers

Pupils' book 4 ☐ A

1 It prevents tooth decay.
2 Probably not; Dr Rich has never heard of anyone dying from a fluoride overdose.
3 You should make them vomit, give them milk or antacid, and take them to hospital.
4 Any two of: in drinking water, as a dietary supplement, in toothpaste.
5 To demonstrate that she is competent to answer the questions.

Pupils' book 4 ☐ B

6 All the sentences containing *if*, plus: *Scientific studies have shown that fluoride can help to prevent cavities as long as it is used correctly.*
7 Answers will vary.

☐ 15A   Conditionals ⚫

Answers will vary. The general format could be: *If you have a coal or wood fire, you need to clean it regularly* or *A gas fire is clean but if you have a coal or wood fire, you need to clean it regularly.*

☐ 15B   Conditionals ⚫

Answers will vary.

Look at these points which were made in a discussion about gas and coal or wood fires. Write one or two sentences to express each one. Remember to use the word *if*.

Gas fire	Coal or wood fire
clean	needs cleaning regularly
can be switched off	dies down
uses gas	can use different fuels
everyone has one	special atmosphere
can control heat	takes time to warm up
cheap to run	expensive
always looks the same	always different
fuel already in the home	fuel must be delivered

Conditionals

You are going away with your aunt and uncle for a weekend. The journey will be about 60 miles (100 kilometres). Consider whether you should travel by car or by train.

If you get stuck, here are some things to consider that might help you:
luggage / speed / parking / traffic / accidents / comfort / refreshment / privacy.

15 Conditionals

In a conditional sentence, a speaker or writer explains what would happen in certain conditions. Conditional sentences:

- have at least two clauses
- often contain the word 'if'
- may contain a modal verb (e.g. *might, should, could*)
- can refer to the past (why or how something happened) or the future (possible consequences).

Here are some examples:

> *If you have a coal fire, you have to clean it regularly.*

> *Most drugs are harmful, unless they are taken as directed.*

> *He might have thought the dog would bite him.*

Notice that you can alter the impact of a conditional sentence by changing the order of the clauses, or by replacing 'if' with a modal verb:

> *If you get a dog, you will have to walk it regularly.*

> *You would have to walk a dog regularly.*

Revision (1) – narrative writing

The purpose of this unit is to allow pupils to pull together all they have learned in previous units, with a particular focus on complex sentences and active/passive verbs, in order to write a longer narrative piece.

NLS coverage

All objectives, with a focus on:

SL 1 To investigate further the use of active and passive verbs

SL 3 To revise work on complex sentences: identifying main clauses; ways of connecting clauses; constructing complex sentences; appropriate use of punctuation

Learned through:

TL Reading comprehension and writing composition
7 To identify the key features of different types of literary text
11 To write own story using, e.g. flashbacks or a story within a story to convey the passing of time
12 To study in depth one genre and produce an extended piece of similar writing

Assessment criteria

SL By the end of this unit, pupils should be able to: identify and model complex sentences; use passive verb forms when appropriate.

TL Writing composition
Children should be able to use typical language features and language of a literary genre to write an extended narrative piece.

Session 1

You will need OHT 16 and PCM 16A.

Shared reading

1 Explain to pupils that you will be working on a longer piece of writing over the next sessions. There is a start to the story, but it's really not very good. Where the story goes after this depends on individual writers.

2 Display and read OHT 16. Can pupils identify the most likely genre? What sort of story will it be? Ask pupils to explain their answers. Most will go for 'mystery' or 'adventure'. How do they know this? The language is not characteristic. It is the plot and the way it is set up. Discuss the way the characters are set out, and what the possible outcomes are. Consider these in the light of 'typical' plots. Refer to other known stories; encourage pupils to use these. Remind them to use books/stories/videos/TV, etc. as inspiration. Other writers do!

Sentence level work

1 The language in this outline is not really characteristic of the genre. Look at the way the sentences are structured. How would pupils describe them? – long/short; simple/complex.

2 Experiment with the first paragraph.
Three children were sitting in a café. There was one girl and two boys.
Look at ways of combining these sentences, then extending them, for example:
A girl and two boys were sitting in a café.
One Sunday afternoon, a girl and two boys were sitting in a café.
One Sunday afternoon in September, Sarah, Jack and Ben sat drinking milkshakes in a café.
One Sunday afternoon in September, Sarah, Jack and Ben sat drinking milkshakes in a café, waiting for Niloofar.

3 Discuss the changes you are making and the impact they have on the text as you write. Discuss common sentence structures; how can you emulate other mystery writers? Refer back to texts with which pupils are familiar. Continue to work on sentences until pupils are confident.

4 As you work, be explicit about punctuation choices and how punctuation relates to sentence structure. For example, look at different possibilities for punctuating the final sentence above.

Independent activities

1 Pupils complete PCM 16A, which allows them to plan the rest of the story. This will be their own story; they will have access to the ideas discussed during shared text work but they can also develop their own ideas.

2 Pupils who finish may continue work on adapting the opening of the story, putting into practice what you have covered on complex sentences.

Plenary

1 Begin by discussing the ending of stories. Remind pupils of the importance of knowing where the story is going, so that you can lay clues for readers. Is everyone happy with the ending of their story? Discuss chosen endings.

2 Ask pupils to share their work on the second paragraph. Write up sentences onto OHT/board and consider punctuation choices. Discuss the impact of pupils' choices, and which seems most appropriate for the genre.

Session 2

You will need pupils' book 4, Unit 16, pages 40–41, and PCM 16B.

Shared reading

1 Explain that the text you will be reading here is called *Prequel*. Is this a term with which pupils are familiar? What might it mean? Discuss other words with similar clusters, e.g. *sequel*.

2 This is a story about something that happened before the story on the OHT, but is connected to it. Ask pupils to turn to page 40 in the pupils' book, and allow them five minutes to read the story. Then read it together. Now, ask pupils for any perceived links between the two stories.

3 Discuss what Samantha might be feeling, or thinking. Look for evidence from the text.

Sentence level work

1 Explain to pupils that the writer has used a mixture of active and passive forms in this story. Begin by selecting a sentence that contains a passive verb form. Focus on the first paragraph:

Samantha <u>was loved</u> by everyone who knew her; she, in turn, loved soccer. She watched soccer, read about soccer, talked about soccer, played soccer. It was her whole life. So when the school team selection <u>was posted</u> – and she was not on it – her world fell apart.

2 Can pupils identify a passive verb form (underlined above)? How do they know that this is a passive form? Very often, in passive forms, the writer is concealing the identity of the agent. However, there are some passives when the writer tells readers who is performing the action.

3 Look at these sentences, and how they differ. In the first one, the writer identifies the agent by using the preposition *by*. In the second sentence, the agent is unclear. Why is this? (Does it matter who posted the selection?) Generate more passive forms using the basic structures given here:

X was Yed by Z   *The X was Yed*

Independent activities

Children complete questions A and B in the pupils' book.

Plenary

Discuss the characters in the story so far. Ask pupils to think of names; guide them away from using names of other pupils in the class. Distribute PCM 16B for homework. Pupils select a main character from their story and complete the outline. This will help them to imagine the character in detail, so that s/he will come to life in the story.

Session 3

You will need pupils' book 4, Unit 16, pages 40–41, and the Reminder Sheet.

Shared writing

Select one of the plots which pupils outlined on PCM 16A in Session 1. Ask the writer about the characters s/he has created. Explain that you will be working on the next section of the story. Invite the writer to join you at the board!

Write together

1 Begin by asking the writer to explain what s/he had envisaged happening in the next part of the story – to flesh out the plan. Work with the writer, helping

him/her to translate ideas into text. Invite contributions from other pupils, and experiment with use of passives / complex sentences.

2 Introduce the Reminder Sheet, which refers to the use of complex sentences and passive forms.

Independent writing activity

Pupils continue with their own writing.

Plenary

Ask other pupils to share their writing. They may need additional time for writing before the final revision/editing session. Discuss what time is available for writing (e.g. homework / timetabled English lessons). Make sure pupils are clear what is expected of them in terms of the length of the piece, and remind them of their personal learning targets.

Session 4

You will need pupils' book 4, Unit 16, pages 40–41, and the Reminder Sheet.

Shared writing

1 Explain that you will now be revising and editing a piece. Look at the options for this – including exchanging writing with another writer for comment.

2 Pupils exchange their writing, and ask for comment on a section with which they are not happy. Allow five minutes for reading and rereading. Then pupils return work and take turns to discuss the section with which they are concerned.

Write together

Invite one pair to share the discussion they have had about one of the pieces. Read the focus section to the rest of the class, and see if they agree with the editor's comments. Revise together, focusing on the use of complex sentences where appropriate.

Independent writing activity

Pupils edit each other's writing, then return it for revision and completion.

Plenary

Discuss possibilities for publication – as a display or as an anthology in a book/website, etc. Decide on a format with which everyone is happy and set a deadline by which final versions will be available.

Assessment

Pupils should be able to:
• expand sentences
• punctuate complex sentences accurately
• identify and compose passive forms
• write an extended narrative piece in the style of a mystery.

Model answers

Pupils' book 4 ☐ A

1 It tells what happened before a story starts.
2 Anger, disappointment, sadness, jealousy, humiliation, etc.
3 Pupils may suggest that Samantha's friends thought she was too embarrassed to come to school, or too angry or depressed.
4 They may have thought she was 'up to something'.
5 Answers will vary.

Pupils' book 4 ☐ B

6 *Samantha was loved by everyone who knew her... // Although supported by her friends and family... // Her homework was not done, and someone else had to walk the dog. // At breaktime, Samantha was left alone.*
7 The passive sentence which reads well is *Samantha was loved by her parents.*

Pupils will write different versions of the sentences. More able pupils may make all of them read well – check that pupils are aware which work and which do not.

☐ 16A and 16B ⊡
Answers will vary.

16A Story outlines

Use this outline to plan the main events of your story. There is space to include any useful words or phrases, and any extra details you feel may help.

Outline	Details	Words/phrases
Orientation		
Problem		
Resolution		
Complication		
Resolution		
Completion		

Use these prompts to help you create characters. Make notes for each of your main characters.

Character	Notes	
Looks	tall / short / hair / skin / eyes / dress	
Sounds	voice / shoes / music	
Smells	perfume / aftershave / food	
Touch	clothes – soft / stiff / material hair – wiry / soft	
Taste	preferences for food / drink / hobbies, etc.	

Complex sentences

Expanding short sentences, or combining them, can give readers a lot of information. For example, the following sentences can be gradually expanded:

- *A girl and two boys were sitting in a café.*
- *One Sunday afternoon, a girl and two boys were sitting in a café.*
- *One Sunday afternoon in September, Sarah, Jack and Ben sat drinking milkshakes in a café.*
- *One Sunday afternoon in September, Sarah, Jack and Ben sat drinking milkshakes in a café, waiting for Niloofar.*

Sentences can be joined in different ways:

- *One Sunday afternoon in September, Sarah, Jack and Ben sat drinking milkshakes while waiting for Niloofar.*

Passive forms

There are two types of passive:

- The individual performing the action is identified:
  Samantha was loved by everyone who knew her.

- The writer does not say who/what is performing the action:
  The school team selection was posted.

Use passive forms when you want to draw attention to whoever or whatever is on the receiving end of the verb, or when it is not important <u>who</u> is acting. This way you don't give unnecessary information to your readers.

Revision (2) – formal writing

The purpose of this unit is to revise work on formal language, and consolidate sentence contraction and conditionals.

NLS coverage

Key objectives

SL 2 To understand features of formal, official language

SL 4 To revise work on contracting sentences

SL 5 To use reading to investigate conditionals and their uses; use these forms to construct sentences which express, e.g. possibilities, hypotheses; explore use of conditionals in past and future, experimenting with transformations, discussing effects

Learned through:

TL **Reading comprehension and writing composition**

15 To recognize how arguments are constructed to be effective, through, e.g. the expression, sequence and linking of points; the provision of persuasive examples, illustrations and evidence; pre-empting or answering potential objections; appealing to the known views and feelings of the audience

18 To construct effective arguments: developing a point logically and effectively; supporting and illustrating points persuasively; anticipating possible objections; harnessing the known views, interests and feelings of the audience; tailoring the writing to formal presentation where appropriate

WL **8** To build a bank of useful terms and phrases for argument

Assessment criteria

SL By the end of this unit, pupils should be able to:

■ identify formality in language; gain control over increasing formality in their own writing
■ make notes by contracting sentences, eliminating unnecessary elements and contracting other parts
■ identify, manipulate and use more complex conditional forms.

TL **Writing composition**

Children should be able to write an effective argument, structuring the piece effectively and demonstrating control of the grammatical elements on which they have been working.

Session 1

You will need OHT 17, photocopies of OHT 17, and PCM 17A.

Shared reading

1 Begin by explaining to pupils that you will be looking at written arguments. Eventually, pupils will be writing an argument on an issue that is probably dear to their hearts – school uniform. After next term they may be moving to a new school, and may need to buy new uniform.

2 For the first session in this unit, however, they will be looking at another issue – how people feel about masts for mobile phones. Begin by asking how many pupils own mobile phones. How many mobile phones does each family possess? It may be interesting to calculate the percentage of mobile phone owners.

3 Now ask who would be happy if their nearest neighbour allowed a phone company to erect a mast just by their wall/fence? Discuss answers.

4 Explain that the text will be an article from a newspaper about masts. Display and read OHT 17. Compare the figures for phone ownership in the class and for their families to the figures quoted in the article.

5 Discuss whether the article is an argument. Is it clear what the writer's view is? It contains arguments on both sides.

6 Consider the way in which the article has been constructed. Look at each paragraph, and identify the main point and purpose of each. For example:
Schools will have an effective veto on the siting of mobile phone masts and councils will have to go through extended planning procedures before they are erected, it was announced yesterday.
Main point: changes to procedures about mobile phone masts
Purpose: introduction

7 Explain that in doing this – identifying the main ideas – pupils have essentially begun to make notes on the piece. This would be what they would wish to record if they needed to refer back to it later on.

Sentence level work

1 Discuss formal official language. Revise the elements of this, for example use of the passive form. Identify passives in this piece, for example: *it was announced yesterday.* Discuss the choice of the passive form here. Who announced it? Further reading suggests Nick Raynsford, but the decision may not have been his. The announcement probably came from a government body. How might a reader check up on the actual detail of the announcement/publication? No reference is given here, but it should be comparatively easy.

2 Now try changing the first sentence into more active forms.
– *Schools will have an effective veto on the siting of mobile phone masts and councils will have to go through extended planning procedures before they are erected, the Government announced yesterday.*
– *Yesterday, the Government announced that schools will have an effective veto on the siting of mobile phone masts and councils will have to go through extended planning procedures before they are erected.*

3 How does the sentence change? Which version do pupils prefer? Notice how, in the first sentence, the word *schools* comes first. Why might this be? What advantage would this have for a newspaper?

4 Continue this process with one or two other examples.

5 Identify key passive phrases which might be used in argument writing, e.g.
■ *it was announced yesterday*
■ *is expected to*
■ *a map... would be made available.*

Independent activities

1 Give each pupil a photocopy of OHT 17 and a copy of PCM 17A. Explain that their task is to make notes on the article which will help them to explain it to their parents/siblings/friends later. They should first read through the text, highlighting important facts, then write notes on PCM 17A. This is constructed as a 'briefing sheet'.

2 Pupils who finish early may reread the article, and highlight/underline any words or phrases they think may be useful for writing arguments.

Plenary

Select pupils to deliver a briefing on the changes to the procedures surrounding the siting of mobile phone masts. Other pupils comment on clarity and cover.

Session 2

You will need pupils' book 4, Unit 17, pages 42–3, and PCM 17B.

Shared reading

1 Begin by explaining that you will be looking at another issue of interest to pupils – school uniforms. Pupils will have plenty of opportunity for airing their views during the course of this unit! Ask who they think may have opinions on whether or not pupils should wear school uniform, e.g. pupils / parents / teachers / governors / public / clothing manufacturers. All of these groups will have different views/slants on the issue.

2 You will be reading an article from a magazine called *Pressgang* which is written by and for schoolchildren in Liverpool.

3 Direct children to page 42 of the pupils' book. Allow five minutes for them to read the article twice. Do pupils agree with all of the points made in the article? There are three issues here: ask pupils to identify them (wearing of uniform / girls wearing trousers / summer uniforms).

4 Now ask pupils to identify the points made in the article which they think are most persuasive, for any of the issues. Allow two minutes' discussion, then share ideas.

5 Ask pupils what they feel about the text. Are there any ideas there which were new to them? Have they changed their minds at all? Do they feel some of these issues would be resolved more easily than others?

6 Look at the people who have been quoted in the article. What do they have in common? (They are all headteachers.) Why do pupils think the writer has interviewed and quoted headteachers rather than pupils or parents? This balance must be redressed!   The focus of the writing will be to explore the issue from another point of view.

Sentence level work

One of the features of the quotes from the headteachers interviewed is the way in which they use sentences which have 'inbuilt' conditionals. These are all complex sentences. Take the opportunity to revise the punctuation and structure of the sentences, identifying the main clause in each case.

– *'As they may be too expensive for some parents, they were to remain as an optional summer outfit.'*
– *'We have never seen any reason to dissuade them from it, as long as they aren't the height of fashion.'*

Independent activities

Children complete questions A and B in the pupils' book.

Plenary

1 Share examples of conditional sentences pupils have composed.

2 Distribute PCM 17B as homework. Encourage pupils to collect responses from different sorts of people, rather than just children.

Session 3

You will need completed version of PCM 17B, and the Reminder Sheet.

Shared writing

1 Ask pupils to share the ideas they have collected from their research. Draw up a table to record:
   ■ the point made
   ■ who made it
   ■ whether it is for or against school uniform.

2 Invite each pupil to contribute one response from their store – the one they think is the best, and to identify who gave it. For each one, see if any others have been given this idea, or a variation of it. Is it for or against school uniform? Ask pupils to record where the idea came from; it will be useful to know which ideas are common to all groups and which are special to particular groups. Go through this as briskly as possible.

Write together

Once all ideas have been collected, discuss which are the most widely held – both for and against. Discuss the importance of structure with pupils – if each idea is the basis of a paragraph, which should come first, which second, etc.?

Independent writing activity

Assign the main ideas to each group to begin writing. They should write two versions of each argument: one as a *pro* and one as a *con*.

Plenary

Organize the exchange of drafts between groups and allow five minutes for quick revision. Collect draft paragraphs from all of the groups and sort them into *pros* and *cons* for the next session.

Session 4

You will need pupils' book 4, Unit 17, pages 42–3, and the Reminder Sheet.

Shared writing

Take one viewpoint – either for or against uniform – and distribute the paragraphs. Ask pupils to read them out. Identify the best order in which these can be tackled. Number the paragraphs.

Write together

Working as a class, compose the opening paragraph and work on the next. Review the language linked with the text type, focusing on use of formal language and conditionals.

Independent writing activity

Pupils complete question 8 in the pupils' book, selecting the ideas they want to use and tackling them in the order they think appropriate. It may be necessary to allocate additional time to writing, including homework time.

Plenary

Pupils share their writing with a partner. They select the most persuasive parts of their partner's writing to share with their partner.

Assessment

Sentence level

Pupils should be able to:

- identify formal language and gain control over increasing formality in their own writing
- make notes by contracting sentences
- identify, manipulate and use more complex conditional forms.

Writing composition

Pupils should be able to comment on the way in which the argument is structured, and the way in which language has been used to reinforce the argument, e.g. use of passive forms, use of names to support arguments, conditionals to help readers consider consequences.

Model answers

Pupils' book 4 ☐ A

1 Answers will vary.
2 For: cool, variety; against: expense.
3 Pupils should suggest that trousers are warmer, more comfortable, less restricting.
4 Answers will vary: fashionable clothes may be more expensive, and get damaged; they may be impractical, distracting, lead to competition, etc.
5 Pupils may be upset if their own clothes are not as fashionable or expensive as other people's.

Pupils' book 4 ☐ B

6 *We have never seen any reason to dissuade them from it, as long as they aren't the height of fashion.* If they aren't the height of fashion, [then] we have never seen any reason to dissuade them from it.
7 Answers will vary.

☐ 17A and 17B 🄿

Answers will vary.

Complete a briefing sheet on mobile phone masts. This should contain all relevant information from the article.

| Date: | Audience: |

Subject:

Source of information:

Main points:

Further information from:

Gathering views

Interview three people you know about whether or not pupils should wear school uniform. Record their views on this sheet.

Name:	Date:

Interviewee: pupil / parent / public / teacher / retailer / other

Views for:	Views against:

Interviewee: pupil / parent / public / teacher / retailer / other

Views for:	Views against:

Interviewee: pupil / parent / public / teacher / retailer / other

Views for:	Views against:

17 Revision (2) – formal writing

R

Writing arguments

Remember to open your piece by explaining what the issues are, then deal with each one, paragraph by paragraph. You may not wish to include all of the issues – part of the success of your writing will depend on your choice of the most powerful points.

It may help if you:

- sequence your ideas carefully. Think about a logical order in which to introduce your points.
- use quotes from people, and give their names and jobs – the more senior the better!
- use formal language which sounds less personal. This can be very persuasive.
- use conditional forms, so that people can think through the issues, and what might happen if changes were made.

UNIT 18

Test preparation (3) – sentences and paragraphs

The purpose of this unit is to reinforce the basic skills of building sentences and paragraphs, linking them in ways which are appropriate to the purpose of the text.

NLS coverage

Key objective

SL 4 To secure control of complex sentences, understanding how clauses can be manipulated to achieve different effects

Learned through:

TL Reading comprehension and writing composition
21 To divide whole texts into paragraphs, paying attention to the sequence of paragraphs and to the links between one paragraph and the next
17, 18 To appraise a text quickly and effectively; to secure the skills of skimming, scanning and efficient reading so that research is fast and effective

Assessment criteria

SL By the end of this unit, pupils should be able to identify the effect created by use of different sentence structures; identify links between sentences and paragraphs; use connective devices to link sentences and paragraphs.

TL Writing composition
Children should be able to write texts that are appropriately paragraphed.

Session 1

You will need OHT 18 and PCM 18A.

Shared reading

1 Explain that the text for the class is an extract from an adventure story by Michael Morpurgo. The book is called *Kensuke's Kingdom* (pronounced 'Kinsky's Kingdom'). Draw attention to the alliteration in the title. What sort of word is *Kensuke's*? It is a possessive form (we know this from the apostrophe), so *Kensuke* must be a noun – probably a proper noun. Who, or what, might Kensuke be?

2 Ask pupils to listen carefully to the reading, and to ask three questions about the text.

3 Display and read OHT 18. Ask for questions, and encourage pupils to answer each other's questions.

4 Discuss the main character. Male or female? Feelings? And what about Stella? Ask pupils to supply details to support their ideas. What has happened, and what may happen next? Would they like to read more of this story?

Sentence level work

1 Explain that you will be looking at how sentences are made up. Ask pupils if they have any observations about how Michael Morpurgo has put sentences together. Ask about any which stand out; discuss why the sentence stands out and what impact it has.

2 Now, select sentences for discussion, for example:
I thought then of the sharks cruising the black water beneath me – scenting me, already searching me out, homing in on me – and I knew there could be no hope.
Look at the parentheses. Challenge pupils to create a sentence with the same structure, based on a familiar experience, perhaps at school.

3 Select other sentences and repeat the exercise, building up complex sentences to match.

4 Now look at shorter sentences, for example at the beginning of the third paragraph. Are these sentences? Why has Morpurgo used them? What effect do they create? Look for other short sentences in the piece and discuss their impact.

Independent activities

Pupils complete PCM 18A, which asks them to complete sentences for different types of story modelled on Morpurgo's sentences.

Plenary

Ask each pupil to select their favourite new sentence and share it with a partner. Each pair / small group rates the selected sentences for structure and effect.

Session 2

You will need pupils' book 4, Unit 18, pages 44–5, and PCM 18B.

Shared reading

1 Explain that the extract is a further episode from the same story. Pupils may find answers to the questions raised in the previous session. Revisit these questions. Remind pupils of skimming and scanning skills, the strategies they might use, e.g. looking for key words (*Stella*); running a finger down the centre of the text; reading from the bottom up. Allow pupils two minutes to skim the text on page 44 in the pupils' book for details.

2 Were previous assumptions correct? Ask pupils what else they have gained from scanning the text. Have they all found the same information? Has the new text raised any more questions?

3 Allow time for pupils to read the text independently. Discuss it with them. What do they think the old man is trying to do? Why does he say fire is bad? Discuss the lead character's feelings.

Sentence level work

1 The focus of this session will be the way in which paragraphs are linked. Talk to pupils about the way in which paragraphs are organized in a narrative (by time sequence). Usually the writer deals with events in the order in which they happen. So, how might the writer of such a narrative link paragraphs? S/he might link them by time (*then, next, suddenly, later that afternoon*, etc.). S/he might also use causal/ logical connectives (*so, however*, etc.).

2 Begin by looking at the purpose of each paragraph in the extract, and where Morpurgo has broken them.

3 For example, the first paragraph describes the old man's appearance. Now look at the second paragraph; there is a significant shift. What is it? It moves on to describe the old man's demeanour.

4 Reread the passage, looking at the purpose of each paragraph and the shift at the beginning of the next. Identify how they've been linked. For example, a number of the linking phrases contain *when*.

Independent activities

Children complete questions A and B in the pupils' book. Use PCM 18B to give further practice.

Plenary

Encourage pupils to look at the sentences at the beginning of paragraphs in the original text. Work with the class, altering the sentences by changing the order of clauses, or breaking them down into shorter sentences and considering the effect.

Session 3

You will need pupils' book 4, Unit 18, pages 44–5, and the Reminder Sheet.

Shared writing

1 Explain that you will be writing a description of a meeting between two characters who have difficulty understanding each other. Discuss possible reasons for the lack of understanding – in this case there was a language barrier. There may also be a sensory difficulty – if one character is deaf, or there is a great age difference.

2 Once you have decided on the difficulty, select your two characters. Remind pupils that the episode you have read has a useful device – the dog understands both characters. Choose a similar 'neutral' character for your episode.

3 Use the paragraph structure of the pupils' book text to structure the writing, e.g. physical description / behaviour description / someone else's reaction.

Write together

1 Begin by writing a physical description of the other character. This is a 'stand alone' episode; it is not necessary to set the scene – we can assume that readers have already understood the situation.

2 When writing, focus on sentence construction. You may wish to use some models from Morpurgo's writing, as pupils did in the first session.

Independent writing activity

Explain to pupils that they have 30 minutes to write, following a basic plan, and there will be time for revision in the next session. They should aim to produce a draft of the entire piece. Remind them at 15 minutes that they have had half of the time. Give another reminder when there are five minutes to go.

Plenary

Very brief: check how many pupils have finished a draft. Did any finish early? What did they do with their spare time? What about those who did not finish: what did they do when there were five minutes left? Select one piece for copying onto OHT for revision.

Session 4

You will need pupils' book 4, Unit 18, pages 44–5, and the Reminder Sheet.

Shared writing

1 Remind pupils they will be revising their drafts.

2 Review focuses for editing: sentence construction and linking paragraphs.

Write together

1 Read aloud the piece selected from the previous session. Explain the importance of reading a piece for revision, to see how it 'sounds'. In a test situation, they will have to read it 'in their heads'. Consider pace and balance – is there too much

detail in any part? Is there enough variation in sentence structure? Could any sentences be joined/split to greater effect? Check punctuation.

2 Now look at the linking phrases. Do they work? Could they be improved? Encourage pupils to read and reread until they are happy with the links.

Independent writing activity

Pupils work in pairs on their texts, focusing on sentence construction and paragraph links.

Plenary

Each pair selects one change with which they're most pleased, and shares with another pair.

Assessment

Pupils should be able to:
• identify and describe different sentence structures, and their impact
• vary sentence structures in their own writing to maintain pace and sustain interest
• link paragraphs in their writing more effectively.

Model answers

Pupils' book 4 ☐ A

1 He might have been relieved to meet someone, or frightened by the old man. Pupils should support their answers from the text.

2 The dog may have met the old man before.

3 The fire might attract attention.

4 He may have been too agitated to speak clearly, or speaking an unknown language.

5 He is showing the boy which part of the island he can go on. This may make the boy feel more lonely, that he is not trusted or welcome.

Pupils' book 4 ☐ B

6 Answers will vary; this is a rough guide:

Para	Purpose	Link to previous para
1	Physical description	Start of description
2	Description of behaviour	Immediate impression
3	Description of dog's behaviour	Boy's response
4	Man speaks	Dialogue
5	Boy speaks	Dialogue
6	Man speaks	Dialogue
7	Boy speaks	Dialogue
8	Man draws map	Man's response

 18A and 18B |₂|

Answers will vary. Check that pupils have followed the instructions.

Here are some sentences from *Kensuke's Kingdom*. Write your own sentences based on these models, one for a ghost story and one for a school story.

	Original sentence	Ghost story	School story
1	The lights of the *Peggy Sue* went away into the dark of the night, leaving me alone in the ocean, alone with the certainty that they were already too far away, that my cries for help could not possibly be heard.		
2	I trod water, frantically searching the impenetrable darkness about me for something, anything to swim towards.		
3	She would keep bobbing away from me, vanishing, reappearing, then vanishing again.		
4	I grabbed it and clung on, feeling the unexpected and wonderful buoyancy of it.		

Sentences from *Kensuke's Kingdom* by Michael Morpurgo (Heinemann Young Books, an imprint of Egmont Children's Books Ltd, 1999) copyright © Michael Morpurgo 1999, reprinted by permission of David Higham Associates.

Building sentences and paragraphs

Here is some text made up of short sentences, with no paragraph breaks. Improve it by varying sentence structure and breaking it into paragraphs. Remember to add linking phrases at the beginning of new paragraphs.

> The girl was about six years old. She had on a blue dress and a white hat. She was tall for her age. She looked upset. She started crying. She cried quietly at first. Then she got louder. 'Calm down, calm down,' I said. She didn't seem to understand. I had a good idea. I said, 'Coca cola?' She stopped crying straight away. She smiled. She took the can and poured some into her mouth. 'Gracias,' she whispered. I wished I could make her understand me. 'Where's your mum?' I asked her. She started crying again. She stood up and took me by the hand. She pulled me along the path.

_____

_____

_____

_____

_____

_____

_____

Paragraph links

When you are writing, make sure you think carefully about planning paragraphs before you start. It is important to break the text when the subject changes, or when there is a shift in pace. Link paragraphs carefully. Here are some of the links Michael Morpurgo uses:

> *I was about to turn and run when...*

> *He was no more than a few feet away from me when...*

> *Instantly...*

Sentence structure

It is important to vary sentence structure, to help the reader. Make sure sentences are not too long, or the reader will get mixed up. Use short sentences for effect. In these two sentences, Michael Morpurgo has used one long sentence and one short one:

> *I thought then of the sharks cruising the black water beneath me – scenting me, already searching me out, homing in on me – and I knew there could be no hope. I would be eaten alive.*

Comparing text types (1) – narrative/recount

The purpose of this unit is to investigate similarities and differences between narrative and recount texts.

NLS coverage

Key objective

[SL] **1** To revise the language conventions and grammatical features of the different types of text, such as narrative (e.g. stories and novels); recounts (e.g. anecdotes, accounts of observations, experiences)

Learned through:

[TL] **Reading comprehension and writing composition**
19 To review a range of non-fiction text types and their characteristics, discussing when a writer might choose to write in a given style and form
22 To select the appropriate style and form to suit a specific purpose and audience, drawing on knowledge of different non-fiction text types

Assessment criteria

[SL] By the end of this unit, pupils should be able to:
- identify use of journalistic style
- appreciate the impact of stylistic features
- use journalistic devices, and description, in their own writing.

[TL] **Writing composition**
Children should be able to understand the difference between narrative fiction and recount which may have features of narrative.

Session 1

You will need OHT 19, recounts from local newspapers, and PCM 19A.

Shared reading

1 Explain that the text will be a newspaper article about a dog. Ask pupils to predict possible angles for a story with this subject. Pupils should explain their suggestions. Make sure they discuss what might be considered 'newsworthy'.

2 Display and read OHT 19.

3 Invite a pupil to read OHT 19 aloud, adopting the intonation of a newscaster. This will help the reader and other pupils identify 'journalistic' features of the text. Ask for further versions from other pupils. Discuss how they knew which bits to emphasize, when to vary their voices and so on.

4 Discuss the appeal of this story. Who might be interested in it? How would the people involved feel?

Sentence level work

1 Distribute whiteboards/paper. Explain to pupils that they should make a note of words, phrases and other features that confirm this is a newspaper report.

2 Allow pupils three minutes to make notes.

3 Identify features of newspaper reports – from layout to language and vocabulary. Discuss which would be the most important features. Investigate the sentences and phrases – which have been chosen by most pupils? How can they be described? Discuss overall sentence length, type of language, use of adjectives, etc. Note also the use of alliteration, and the way in which the writer has included details about the main protagonists without actually describing them. Why is age so important? Draw up a list of features of newspaper recounts.

Independent activities

1 Distribute copies of PCM 19A. Pupils check the features of newspaper recounts and add any additional ones from the class investigation.

2 Distribute newspaper recounts. Pupils should check at least two against the list of features.

Plenary

Discuss pupils' findings. Referring to the checklist, identify any differences which might be found between articles on the front page and inside pages of a newspaper. Consider: appeal and perceived importance; size of headline/photograph/font; experience of journalist.

Session 2

You will need pupils' book 4, Unit 19, pages 46–7, and PCM 19B.

Shared reading

1 This is another story involving dogs – but of quite a different kind! Explain to pupils that you will be asking them to decide what type of text it is, and to give evidence for their decisions.

2 Turn to page 46 of the pupils' book and read the text aloud. Allow pupils two minutes to consider the genre, and select evidence to support their decision. Share ideas. Discuss the level of consensus – it should be fairly high. Look at the range of evidence selected. Ask pupils to decide what evidence they think is most persuasive.

3 Ask for responses to the story itself. What sort of place does Hades seem to be? Does anyone know what it is? Explain the role of Hades in Greek mythology, and the role of Cerberus.

Sentence level work

1 Discuss the differences between the two 'dog' texts. Focus particularly on the language. Ask pupils to look at the level of description, and the types of description. The writer of this story has used a lot of figurative language. Explain that 'figurative' language helps readers/listeners to imagine what something is like. It includes use of adjectives and adverbs, as well as simile and metaphor.

2 Select one description, e.g.

… a pair of gates a mile high, the spiked points rising higher than the mountain, brushing the very clouds. The gates were made of black iron, with iron skulls set between the twisting bars.

How does the writer want us to feel about these gates? He wants us to feel what Orpheus must have felt, so he uses description to emphasize the

size and horror of the gates. They reach right to the sky – into the clouds! Is this exaggeration, or not? It doesn't matter – it is a story. This is a magical place, anything could be true. The gates have iron skulls between the bars. Why has the being who made the gates put in skulls? What image do they give, what might they represent?

3 Discuss why the writer has said that the bars are *twisting*. Experiment with reading the sentence aloud without the adjective. It doesn't sound right – an adjective is required for the type of story this is.

Independent activities

Children complete questions A and B in the pupils' book. Offer PCM 19B to those who might struggle with questions 6 and 7.

Plenary

Discuss selections of text, and reasons for them. Invite two pupils to share their versions of the sentences; others should offer positive suggestions.

Session 3

You will need pupils' book 4, Unit 19, pages 46–7, OHT 19, and the Reminder Sheet.

Shared writing

1 Explain to pupils that over the next two sessions they will be working on 'genre exchange'. The two genre / text types involved are journalistic recount and myth.

2 Begin with rewriting the Hades story as a newspaper report. Review the features of newspaper recounts. Discuss how long the piece should be – refer back to OHT 19 for a reminder.

Write together

1 Begin with a headline for the story, e.g.
Youth tames freak beast.
Cerberus defeated by lyre.

2 Invite pupils to offer suggestions. Discuss each one and decide on the selection.

3 Continue with the first few sentences. Model the use of journalistic devices and phraseology. Discuss and, where appropriate, accept suggestions and contributions. Look at how much shorter the piece is. Look at what has not been included.

Independent writing activity

Pupils continue the story, with reference to the Reminder Sheet. Work with a group who may have difficulty reducing the length of the original.

Plenary

Allow pupils to exchange stories and offer two 'editing' suggestions.

Session 4

You will need pupils' book 4, Unit 19, pages 46–7, and the Reminder Sheet.

Shared writing

In this session, you will be writing the story of Kaske as a myth. Review the features you will be looking for. Can this dog be made into a fantastical beast? Build up the angle of the story – how will it be told? From whose point of view? Remember that this story will be longer than the newspaper original. What must be added?

Write together

1 Begin by writing brief descriptions – of the dog, the toddler and the lake. Use passages from the myth text as models.

2 Now begin to build up the story. Write the first paragraph, with a description of the park and lake. Map out the rest of the story.

Independent writing activity

Pupils continue to write – referring to the Reminder Sheet for features.

Plenary

Pupils identify the best parts of their rewritten story, and share it with a partner. Discuss why they chose it.

Assessment

Reading comprehension

Pupils should be able to identify genre / text type, and select evidence for their view; understand what is meant by 'figurative language' and identify figurative language in texts they read.

Writing composition

Pupils should be able to use features of imaginative narrative and journalistic recount in their writing. Comment on the extent to which they have successfully adopted stylistic features and structure.

Model answers

Pupils' book 4 ▱ A

1 Myth.
2 The gates were a mile high.
3 Orpheus was quite calm; he moved slowly and did not panic.
4 Answers will vary; pupils should give supporting evidence.
5 To make sure the dog was asleep, for his own satisfaction.

Pupils' book 4 ▱ B

6 Choices will vary. Check that pupils can identify simile and metaphor.
7 Pupils should use the same structure as the model sentences.

▱ 19A and 19B   Comparing text types (1) – narrative/recount ▯

Answers will vary. Check that pupils have understood the features of recount and narrative.

Comparing text types (1) – narrative/recount

Newspaper recounts

First of all, check the features of newspaper recounts below. If you can think of any additional ones, add them.

Next, check whether each article has these features. Write down any good examples.

Feature	Article 1	Article 2	Article 3
Headline			
Photograph			
Sub-headings			
Names			
Details of people			
Recount of events			
Quotations			
Bystanders' comments			
Emotional language			
Conclusion / writer comment			
'Journalistic' language – examples			
Other features			

Comparing text types (1) – narrative/recount

Here are some phrases and sentences from the text. Explain why you think the writer has chosen them, and then write a sentence of your own in the same style. Finish off the one that is started, or write your own.

Original words	Why they work well	My own words
The gates were made of black iron, with iron skulls set between the twisting bars.		The door was made of …
… an enormous cavern, a great circle of darkness.		… a _____ lake, …
The dog was huge, bigger than a horse. Its black fur hung in knots off its deformed body as if it had rolled in tar.		The cat was …

19 Comparing text types (1) – narrative/recount

Features of newspaper reports

Headline

Photograph

Sub-headings

Names

Details of people

Recount of events

Quotations

Bystanders' comments

Emotional language

Conclusion / writer comment

'Journalistic' language

Features of myths

Fantastic creatures

Magic/mystery

Descriptive language: adjectives and adverbs

careful selection of nouns and verbs

similes

metaphors

UNIT 20 — Comparing text types (2) – report/explanation

The purpose of this unit is to investigate similarities and differences between report and explanation texts. Pupils will examine examples of the text types, contrast them, and write an explanation which contains definitions, as might be found in a report.

NLS coverage

Key objective

SL 1 To revise the language conventions and grammatical features of report and explanatory texts

Learned through:

TL Reading comprehension and writing composition
15 To secure understanding of the features of explanatory texts from Year 5 term 2
19 To review a range of non-fiction text types and their characteristics, discussing when a writer might choose to write in a given style and form
22 To select the appropriate style and form to suit a specific purpose and audience, drawing on knowledge of different non-fiction text types

Assessment criteria

SL By the end of this unit, pupils should be able to distinguish between report and explanatory texts; use grammatical features of these texts in their own writing.

TL Writing composition
Children should be able to write reports and explanations using appropriate style and form.

Session 1

You will need OHT 20 and PCM 20A.

Shared reading

1 Introduce the unit by explaining that the class will be looking at two texts relating to hills and mountains. Although both hills and mountains are dangerous, it is for different reasons. Allow pupils one minute to think of reasons why hills and mountains could be dangerous. They should write down two reasons.

2 Have any pupils ever visited Silbury Hill? If so, ask them to recap briefly what they remember, and what makes it special. Display and read OHT 20.

3 Look at the text in some detail. Why is this hill dangerous? Ask pupils who had thought of this particular reason to hold up their hands.

4 Go through the information in detail. Could anyone draw an outline of Silbury Hill from the information given here? What is the most interesting fact about the hill? Can pupils speculate as to the possible reason for the hill being built?

5 Look at the structure of the text. Identify the purpose of each paragraph. Note that there is an introduction, and paragraphs devoted to specific aspects. Try thinking up headings for each paragraph.

Sentence level work

1 What type of text is this? The structural analysis should have given a clue – it is a report. Review with pupils the features of a report. In general, they should know that:
- the organization of reports is not chronological
- reports are written in the present tense
- the focus is on generic rather than specific phenomena.

2 Review each of these in the light of the text about Silbury Hill. Make sure pupils notice that the text is organized by time, but not chronology. The first paragraph is about the mound today, then it goes to the possible origins of the mound, and then returns to current problems.

The predominant tense is the present. However, there are examples of use of other tenses. Ask pupils to find these.

Independent activities

Pupils complete PCM 20A. They need to reorganize the statements into an appropriate sequence, and then link them to make a good non-chronological report.

Plenary

Focus on the structure and the language used. Begin by asking pupils how many paragraphs they have used for their report. Review the importance of paragraphing. Look at their reports, paragraph by paragraph. Discuss how ideas are organized into paragraphs.

Session 2

You will need pupils' book 4, Unit 20, pages 48–9.

Shared reading

1 Explain to pupils that you will be reading another text about hills/mountains – this time, naturally occurring ones. Ask them what they know about volcanoes. This text is about how volcanoes erupt. If this is the purpose of the text, what sort of text do they predict it will be?

2 Ask pupils to turn to page 48 in the pupils' book. Do any of them recognize the style of writing and presentation of this particular text?

3 Read and discuss the text – do pupils feel it helps them to understand what happens with volcanoes? Divide the pupils into pairs, and allow them some time to explain the process to each other. Check that they have the facts correct.

4 Discuss what it is about the text that pupils think makes it easy/difficult to understand.

Sentence level work

1 Allow pupils three minutes to read the text to themselves. Ask them to make a note of any features they would have expected, and anything that was unexpected.

2 Look at the features of explanatory texts. How formal was this text? What was the predominant tense? Look at connectives, and identify which type of connectives are which.

3 Consider things that make this explanation different from others they may have expected – for example, the informal tone, the use of examples (e.g. the parallel with the pop can).

4 Discuss also how useful the illustrations are in relation to the text. Look at the language in the diagram label.

5 Discuss differences between reports and explanations. Remind pupils that these texts answer different questions: reports tell us <u>what</u>; explanations tell us <u>why</u> or <u>how</u>. Consider also the time sequence in explanations. Some reports include this (for example, in history). Note language features, e.g. use of present tense.

Independent activities

Children complete questions A and B in the pupils' book.

Plenary

Discuss pupils' collections of connectives – have they classified them correctly? What are the areas of disagreement? Discuss issues.

Session 3

You will need pupils' book 4, Unit 20, pages 48–9, PCM 20B, and the Reminder Sheet.

Shared writing

Explain to pupils that you are going to be writing up a more formal explanation of how a volcano erupts. Discuss the information already available – in the pupils' book text. Is there sufficient detail there? What other detail might be included? How might this information be accessed? List possible sources of information. Draw up a grid for mapping out information (see PCM 20B). The same numerical stages will help pupils who are unsure. Make notes onto an OHT version of this from the pupils' book text.

Write together

Ask pupils how to translate the information in the model text into notes for the planning sheet. Demonstrate writing concise notes – discuss lack of punctuation, limits to amount of information to be included, and so on. Remind pupils that notes such as this are written to aid memory. They may be used for revision purposes, or form the basis of a later piece of writing, as in this case. It will be important to include enough detail so that the writer can remember what s/he meant!

Independent writing activity

Pupils consult other sources, and add information to PCM 20B for later discussion.

Plenary

Collect information from all pupils' research efforts; gather it onto an OHT version of PCM 20B.

Session 4

You will need the completed PCM 20B, and the Reminder Sheet.

Shared writing

1 Begin by planning out the main stages – from formation of the volcano to eruption. Discuss the timescale: how relevant is this to the eruption? Should this sort of detail be included?

2 Discuss the format of an explanation – you will be focusing on the body of the explanation; some pupils may wish to add an introduction and conclusion to this.

Write together

Begin writing, using details identified in the previous session. Demonstrate use of time sequence for paragraphing. Discuss the level of formality required – range of sentence types, use of present tense, and so on. Draw pupils' attention to different ways of giving information through use of technical vocabulary. Definitions of words can be included, or sentences can be constructed to show what words mean.

Independent writing activity

Pupils begin writing their own version of the explanation. More able pupils may wish to include elements such as an introduction and conclusion.

Plenary

Review some pupils' work. Discuss pictorial support: what would be helpful; what would be distracting?

Assessment

Pupils should be able to:
- differentiate between report and explanatory texts
- identify connectives and other stylistic features relevant to both forms
- use these features in their own writing
- write a simple explanatory text, using features identified from their own reading.

Model answers

Pupils' book 4 ◿ A

1 Explanation.
2 It helps readers to understand what happens.
3 Aimed at children – the language and format suggest this.
4 Uses clear steps, simple language, detail, e.g. experiment, diagrams.
5 Answers will vary.

Pupils' book 4 ◿ B

6 Instruction.
7 All the features are found in this text, except 'formal voice'. The title acts as an introduction.
8 time: *as, until, eventually*; logic: *because, so*

20A   Comparing text types (2) – report/ explanation ▯

This is a difficult exercise and answers will vary. You may wish to help pupils put the points in a suitable order, or at least check they have done so before they start writing the report.

20B   Comparing text types (2) – report/ explanation ▯

Stage	Main point	Extra detail
1	Magma rises	
2	Pressure begins	
3	Pressure builds	
4	Magma and gases erupt	
5	Lava is formed, and cools hard	

Avebury

Here are some facts about Avebury Henge.

Reorganize them so they are in a good sequence.
(Numbering them is a good way to start.)

Link them to construct a report about the site.

	The Avebury stones are about 30 million years old.
	A Saxon church was built in Avebury in about AD 850.
	Avebury Henge was built around 2500 BC – that's 4500 years ago.
	The people who lived in the area were farmers. They could make tools and pottery, and probably decorated their bodies.
	Avebury contains: the largest stone circle (henge) in Europe; one of the longest burial mounds (or barrows) in Europe; an avenue of standing stones; and Silbury Hill – the largest pre-historic mound in Europe.
	There is now a museum at Avebury.
	When Avebury Henge was built, nobody could write. This is why we do not know exactly how it came to be built.
	Some stones have been replaced to show people what it would have looked like.
	At least 30 people are buried in West Kennet Long Barrow.
	Avebury Henge had four entrances and two inner circles.
	The ditch around the henge was dug out with deer antlers and shoulder blades from cattle.
	The ground underneath is white chalk.
	One of the stones has disappeared – even though it probably weighed about 60 tonnes.

This will help you gather and sort information for your explanation. Use it to record facts, and plan your writing.

Stage	Main point	Extra detail
1	Magma rises	
2		
3		
4		
5		

Non-chronological reports describe things. They have this structure:

Feature	Example
An opening statement or classification	Silbury Hill in Wiltshire is the largest man-made mound in all of Europe.
Paragraphs describing different parts of the object	It must have taken about 35 million baskets of chalk rubble and earth, and up to a hundred years to build.
A closing statement	Silbury has dominated the landscape for almost 5000 years.

Reports are usually written in the present tense, but sometimes the writer will use the past tense or the future tense. For example:

Silbury Hill is a site of special scientific interest.

We know that it was started in late summer.

It may be possible to repair Silbury Hill, using a helicopter.

Explanatory texts tell us how or why something happens. They have this structure:

Feature	Example
An general introduction (sometimes the title)	How on Earth do volcanoes erupt?
A series of logical steps	2 The magma rises into the crust… 3 And up… and up. 4 … until, one day, the magma…
The final step/summary	Eventually, it cools and becomes solid cold rock.

Explanations are often written in the simple present tense. They use connectives that signal time or causal connectives. For example:

… <u>until</u>, one day, the magma and gas rush upwards, burst out through cracks in the crust, and erupt.

It rises <u>because</u> it's mixed with gas <u>so</u> it's lighter than the rocks around it.

Comparing text types (3) – instruction/explanation

The purpose of this unit is to investigate similarities and differences between instruction and explanatory texts.

NLS coverage

Key objective

SL 1 To revise the language conventions and grammatical features of instructional and explanatory texts

Learned through:

TL **Reading comprehension and writing composition**
15 To secure understanding of the features of explanatory texts from Year 5 term 2
19 To review a range of non-fiction text types and their characteristics, discussing when a writer might choose to write in a given style and form
22 To select the appropriate style and form to suit a specific purpose and audience, drawing on knowledge of different non-fiction text types

Assessment criteria

SL By the end of this unit, pupils should be able to:
- identify explanations and instructions
- understand the key language features of these text types
- use an impersonal form when writing explanations
- use the imperative form in writing instructions.

TL **Writing composition**
Children should be able to write explanations of processes with which they are familiar; write detailed instructions.

Session 1

You will need a sheet of A4 paper and four paperclips for each pupil, OHT 21 and PCM 21A.

Shared reading

1 Introduce the text by discussing paper craft with pupils. There are many things that can be made from paper – even boats! Can pupils think of other things – e.g. hats, planes. Ask how many have ever made a paper plane? How did they learn how to do this? It is likely that most pupils who can make paper planes will have been shown how to do this by someone else. Has anyone ever seen written instructions?

2 Distribute paper to all pupils. Explain that they must try to make the plane as you read the instructions.

3 Begin reading, and allow pupils time to complete each instruction.

4 Discuss how effective these instructions are. Focus in particular on the language, and the level of detail. Ask pupils to whom they think the text is addressed; who did the writer think would be making the aeroplane?

Sentence level work

1 Review the features of instructional texts. Discuss aspects of layout, including sections and use of diagrams/photographs, and language features. Remind pupils that the writer has used the imperative form. Ask if any can remember three features of imperative verbs – allow time to study the text. Make sure that pupils are clear that they are in the second person, present tense, and the verb phrase occurs at the beginning of the sentence. Verbs are sometimes preceded by adverbs – either temporal connectives (*next, first, once the dough has risen*) or more obvious adverbs (*gently, briskly*).

2 Experiment with alternative ways of framing instructions from the shared text. Pupils may use whiteboards for their own versions of sentences.

Independent activities

Using PCM 21A, pupils work on a recount to transform it into a set of instructions for a science experiment. They can complete this for homework. It may be possible to scan the text so that pupils can manipulate it electronically.

Plenary

Gather initial attempts; ask pupils to comment on the progress they have made with the text. Revisit the layout and grammatical conventions previously discussed, and check that these texts conform to those. Suggest that pupils might like to try the activity for homework.

Session 2

You will need pupils' book 4, Unit 21, pages 50–51, and PCM 21B.

Shared reading

1 Ascertain which pupils tried out the activity. Do not spend too much time on results – ask them to bear them in mind while they look at the explanation text for this session.

2 Ask children to turn to page 50 of the pupils' book. Read the explanation text to the class, and discuss it. First of all, check that pupils understand the basic principles, such as the opposite actions of forces on the paper. Check that this description of what happens agrees with the experiences of pupils who carried out the activity. Ask pupils if they can re-formulate these concepts in their own words; challenge other pupils to evaluate their rewordings.

3 Discuss the intended audience for this piece. Draw pupils' attention to its tone, use of informal voice, selection of examples, etc.

Sentence level work

1 Ask pupils to list the features of explanatory texts which are exemplified in this particular text. Are there any that are missing? Any unusual features? If pupils do not notice the use of the imperative form, draw their attention to it. Discuss why the writer has chosen to use the imperative form here.

2 Focus specifically on the use of the second person informal voice and the more formal tone. Help pupils to identify examples of each. Try rewording these sentences in a different voice – more or less

formal. Experiment with different versions; ask pupils for feedback about how different sentences fit in with the rest of the text, how clear they are and how suitable for different groups.

Independent activities

Children complete questions A and B in the pupils' book. Offer PCM 21B to pupils who need additional support.

Plenary

Ask pupils to report on which type of sentence they find easiest to write, and think why. Do different pupils have different preferences? Discuss how this relates to their own individual writing style.

Session 3

You will need pupils' book 4, Unit 21, pages 50–51, and the Reminder Sheet.

Shared writing

1 Explain that you will be writing an explanation text. Remind pupils that an explanation text answers the question *how?* or *why?* Consider what might be a suitable subject for a class text, and make a list of topics from which pupils can select to write their own explanations. These should be processes that are familiar to pupils, so that time is not spent on the factual content.

2 Identify an audience for the explanation (younger children / parents / peers), and a publishing opportunity (assembly/newsletter/display). Consider the implications of this choice.

Write together

Review the structure of the explanation text in the pupils' book. Identify the purpose of each paragraph. Remind pupils that the opening paragraph invites readers to consider a question. Model the opening paragraph. Remind pupils that they can use the second person to engage readers' interest. Experiment with a number of possibilities – see how appropriate they are for the purpose and audience.

Independent writing activity

1 Pupils write the opening paragraph of their own explanation. Encourage them to craft this as finely as possible. It is important, as it will determine whether or not readers carry on reading.

2 Pupils who complete the opening paragraph to their own satisfaction may continue with the next section of the explanation.

Plenary

Revise the features of explanatory texts – reminding pupils about effective use of the second person. Have any of them used an imperative form? Collect and discuss texts you have encountered.

Session 4

You will need pupils' book 4, Unit 21, pages 50–51, a completed draft, and the Reminder Sheet.

Shared writing

Explain that you have completed your draft and wish to work on revision and proof-reading. Remind pupils that it is often useful to revisit a text at some distance after initial writing, or to invite others to reflect on it and then try to see it through their eyes. Read the completed draft to the pupils.

Write together

Work on revision, taking pupils' contributions. Demonstrate the use of editing marks. It may be useful to demonstrate how the 'tracking changes' facility on a word processor actually uses the same marks, and identifies changes in red. Why is this helpful?

Independent writing activity

Pupils complete and revise their own explanations.

Plenary

Prepare pieces for publication – either in the format discussed, or for sharing in other ways, e.g. with parents and carers. Pupils identify aspects of which they are most proud in these pieces of writing.

Assessment

In feedback to pupils, focus on the extent to which they:
- are able to identify instructions and explanations
- understand the features of these text types
- write instructions and explanations, using the grammatical features of each
- vary features (e.g. use of second person in explanations) where appropriate.

Model answers

Pupils' book 4 ☐ A

1 Explanation – it explains how something happens.
2 Child – simple, direct language and vocabulary.
3 It exerts a downward force.
4 Answers will vary.
5 Pupils should draw a parallel between the parachute and the flat sheet of paper – surface area and air resistance.

Pupils' book 4 ☐ B

6 The first paragraph and the final sentence are in the second person; the rest are impersonal.

7 Choices will vary.
8 Use of the second person engages the reader initially; the impersonal form is more precise, and appropriate for science and explanation; the final sentence is in the second person, and invites the reader to think about what they have read.

☐ **21A   Writing instructions ⏹**
Check that pupils have included the features of instructions in their writing.

☐ **21B   Comparing text types (3) – instruction/ explanation ⏹**
Answers will vary.

 # *Writing instructions*

Adam has written an account of a science activity. You and your friends could carry out this activity – then rewrite it as a set of instructions.

Experiment

Ms Arlsen told us we needed to work in pairs. Each pair got three pieces of A4 paper for an experiment. It didn't seem like much!

We had to do different things with each piece of paper. One had to be left flat, one had to be folded as small as possible, and one had to be screwed up into a ball.

After that, we had to draw round each piece of paper on some squared paper and work out how many squares it took up. The flat one had the most – we didn't have to draw around that, and the folded one had the least. We got it really small.

Once we'd finished and recorded all of that, we had to see how long each one took to drop. To make it fair we had to drop them from the same height. One of us had a stopwatch, and the other held the paper next to a particular place by the wall – so each one would go as far. We did each one twice, just to make sure there was enough data.

When we had all the information we shared the data and tried to find reasons for our results. Then we thought of real-life situations that worked in the same way. It was quite a good lesson after all!

Complete the table, rewriting each sentence as appropriate.

Second person / Informal	Impersonal
They don't drop at the same rate, do they?	Parachutes don't drop at the same rate.
Can you think of anything else?	Is anything Are there other reasons.
The less surface area an object has, the faster it falls – right?	
	There is more than one force acting on falling objects.
	To understand this, it is necessary to work out which object took longest to fall.
	This is a very important principle – it explains how parachutes work.

21 Comparing text types (3) – instruction/explanation

Instructions are laid out so as to be easy to follow. There are clear sections covering equipment and materials, followed by steps that are often numbered. There may be illustrations or diagrams to help the reader.

Instructions are written in the imperative form. Imperative verbs and verb phrases:
- are in the second person
- are in the present tense
- occur at the beginning of the sentence.

The verbs are sometimes preceded by adverbs – either temporal connectives (*next, first, once [the dough has risen]*) or more obvious adverbs (*gently, briskly*).

In the **explanation** you have read, the writer has mixed informal with formal language.
- Informal
  The less surface area an object has, the faster it falls – right?
  Can you think of anything else?
  (Both these examples are written in the second person – they talk to the reader directly.)
- Formal
  To understand this, it is necessary to work out which object took longest to fall.
  (This example is written in the passive.)

If you decide to mix these different types of writing, be very careful about how you do it. Look back at the model text to give you some ideas.

Formal language (2)

The purpose of this unit is to investigate formal styles of writing. Pupils will practise use of the impersonal voice and passive form, looking at when this is appropriate. They will also experiment with complex sentences.

NLS coverage

Key objective

SL 3 To revise formal styles of writing:
- the impersonal voice
- the use of the passive
- management of complex sentences

Learned through:

TL Reading comprehension and writing composition
16 To identify the key features of impersonal formal language, e.g. the present tense, the passive voice, and discuss when and why they are used
20 To secure control of impersonal writing, particularly the sustained use of the present tense and the passive voice
22 To select the appropriate style and form to suit a specific purpose and audience, drawing on knowledge of different non-fiction text types

Assessment criteria

SL By the end of this unit, pupils should be able to identify features of formal language; manipulate and recreate these features; begin to use these features in their own writing.

TL Writing composition
Children should be able to write using a formal voice, selecting features appropriate to their audience and purpose.

Session 1

You will need OHT 22 and PCM 22A.

Shared reading

1 Explain to pupils that you will be reading an extract from 'The Children's Manifesto'. Do any of them know what a 'manifesto' is? Explain the importance of a manifesto to political parties. What might a 'Children's Manifesto' be? What might it include? Who might have written it? Who might read it? Ask pupils to list the issues they think are important for children.

2 Display and read OHT 22. Review it in the light of pupils' predictions. Make sure that pupils understand all of the text – it is quite challenging.

3 Discuss the ideas in the document; do pupils agree with all of the suggestions?

Sentence level work

1 Ask pupils whether they think children wrote this manifesto? Do they think children are the intended audience? Why? Discuss the formality of the language. Why is the language formal? Review the main features of formal language: use of the present tense, the impersonal voice; the use of the passive; complex sentences.

2 Identify these features in the text:
- Present tense – *are*
- Impersonal language – note the use of general terms, e.g. *children, neighbourhoods, local authorities, community life*
- Passives – *Children and young people <u>are rarely asked</u> about what they need from their communities. If <u>they are denied</u> a role in community life, young people will continue to be disillusioned with, and dismissive of, politics, government and the democratic process.*
- Complex sentences – *Fear of violence and crime, based on the grim reality of bullying at school and*

assaults in the community, concern about drugs and the danger of traffic are key factors in this change.

Children need to be able to take part in decisions made about their own environment, to help with plans for safe housing, traffic-free streets, play and leisure facilities, accessible shops and safe open spaces.

3 Ask pupils which of these features they find most difficult to understand – which one makes reading the text harder? Why? Note how passive forms are often more complex than active ones.

4 How could a formal text like this be simplified for other readers?

Independent activities

Direct more able readers to PCM 22A; less able readers to PCM 22B. All pupils work in pairs, using highlighters to identify features of formal language. Once they have completed this, they make notes to identify the key ideas in the text.

Plenary

Gather the main ideas from the text. Discuss ideas. Which features of formal language did pupils find in the PCMs?

Session 2

You will need pupils' book 4, Unit 22, pages 52–3

Shared reading

1 Explain to pupils that you will be working on another section of 'The Children's Manifesto'.

Together, look at page 52 in the pupils' book. What do pupils notice about the layout? Does this make any difference to the way in which they view the text? Does it look easier or more difficult? Does it affect their confidence in reading the text?

2 Allow pupils four minutes to read the text themselves, then have individual pupils read out the separate sections.

3 Discuss the ideas in the text. Do pupils agree with them? What about the solutions? Would these work?

Sentence level work

1 Focus on the active and passive. Find examples of passive forms in the text, and transform them into active. What impact does this have on the sentences in which they are found?

2 Experiment with transforming sentences from active to passive, for example:
You make the problems.
The problems are made by you.

3 Refer back to PCM 22A/B. Work with sentences taken from these texts.

Independent activities

Children complete questions A and B in the pupils' book.

Plenary

Focus on sentence transformations; ask how many versions of sentences the class has generated. Gather the different versions. Which work well?

Session 3

You will need pupils' book 4, Unit 22, pages 52–3, and the Reminder Sheet.

Shared writing

1 Refer back to the pupils' book text. Look at its structure. What do the three sections of the text do? Make sure pupils understand that the writers have: described a problem, used a quotation to emphasize it, and offered some solutions. Explain that you will be using this structure to write sections for a Class Manifesto.

2 Identify issues about which pupils feel strongly; select one for shared writing, and allocate other issues to groups.

Write together

1 Begin by plotting out the page/board/OHT into three sections. Work on the description of the issue. Divide it into major areas; demonstrate that writers cannot include all aspects of a problem – they have to be selective. Support pupils in framing contributions. Use the passive form, as in the model texts.

2 Discuss how the original quotation might have been derived (from interviews, etc.). How might a quotation be obtained for this manifesto? Work on a quotation for this section, expressing the same sentiments in the language of the pupils.

Independent writing activity

Pupils work in groups on descriptions of their own sections. Work with groups who require additional support or challenge.

Plenary

Arrange for pupils to exchange sections for comment.

Session 4

You will need pupils' book 4, Unit 22, pages 52–3, and the Reminder Sheet.

Shared writing

Continue working on the text, using the bullet point format. Generate ideas, then sort them into an appropriate sequence.

Write together

Begin with the opening sentence of the list. Use the model text as a basis. Then transform ideas into bullet points. Note the layout of bullet points, drawing pupils' attention to the use of a colon to introduce a list. There are some differences, however: semi-colons would normally be used at the end of each point, and there is capitalization. Rules surrounding this seem to be less strict than they were! The list can be viewed as one long sentence, therefore bullet points should really not begin with capitals as if they were a new sentence. Explain to pupils that many word processing applications supply capitals automatically, so this is found quite frequently.

Independent writing activity

Pupils continue drafting in groups, and then work on revisions together. Additional time may be useful to publish this as a manifesto.

Plenary

Discuss a possible location for the completed manifesto – share with the rest of the school in assembly, place in the library, send copies home, etc. What do pupils feel would be appropriate? Arrange for final editing and proof-reading, and set dates for publication.

Assessment

Pupils should be able to:
- identify features of formal language
- use some features of formal language in their own writing, e.g. the passive form (NB some pupils will need support)
- revise and edit texts they have written, identifying weaknesses and remedying them.

Model answers

Pupils' book 4 ◻ A

1 The writers may have thought that this sums up the situation for readers. The speaker's anger and accusation demands attention. Pupils may give other explanations.
2 Answers will vary.
3 Answers will vary.
4 Children may refer to lack of transport and other facilities, relatively small social groups, lack of access to shops, cinemas, etc.
5 Pupils will offer their own interpretations.

Pupils' book 4 ◻ B

6 Sentences will vary. Pupils should understand that the passive voice emphasizes that children are victims in these situations.
7 It presents shocking information in a factual, scientific, unemotional way. This gives the information authority and makes it more believable.
8 Answers will vary.

◻ 22A and 22B   Formal language (2) ◻

Check that pupils have identified the formal language and main ideas in both versions.

Work in pairs, using highlighter pens to identify features of formal language. Then make a list of the key ideas in the text.

The Children's Manifesto

A healthy childhood is the foundation of a healthy adult life. Habits formed in childhood have a long-term impact on health and wellbeing. Yet children are increasingly inactive and overweight, leaving them vulnerable to developing illnesses including heart disease in later life.

Children's health needs are different from those of adults. This should be reflected in the services provided for them. Young people with mental health problems are often cared for on adult wards because there is nowhere else for them. Young people, children with disabilities and those from minority ethnic communities are less likely to use available services. A growing number of children have complex health needs.

We must have co-ordinated services in hospitals and the community. Child and adolescent mental health services should be strengthened to ensure that help is available for children if necessary, independent of their families, at an early stage, before problems become more acute. The physical and emotional health of children looked after by local authorities needs to be given greater priority by social services. Children who are frequently admitted to hospital should have the right to play and education while they are there.

_____

_____

_____

_____

From *Our children, their future – A manifesto* by Barnardo's/Child Poverty Action Group/NSPCC from www.nspcc.org.uk/childrensmanifesto, reprinted by permission of National Society for the Prevention of Cruelty to Children.

Work in pairs, using highlighter pens to identify features of formal language. Then make a list of the key ideas in the text.

The Children's Manifesto

A healthy childhood leads to a healthy adult life. Habits formed in childhood have a long-term impact on health. But more children are lazy and overweight, so they could develop illnesses like heart disease when they are older.

Children have different health needs from adults. This should be reflected in the services provided for them. Young people with mental health problems have to stay on adult wards because there is nowhere else for them. Young people, children with disabilities and those from minority ethnic communities are less likely to use services. More and more children have complex health needs.

We need services in hospitals and the community to work together. Children's mental health services should be made better. This would mean that there is help for children before problems get bigger. The health of children looked after by local authorities needs more attention. Children who have to go into hospital a lot should have the right to play and education while they are there.

_____

_____

_____

_____

Adapted from *Our children, their future – A manifesto* by Barnardo's/Child Poverty Action Group/NSPCC from www.nspcc.org.uk/childrensmanifesto, reprinted by permission of National Society for the Prevention of Cruelty to Children.

22 *Formal language (2)*

Features of formal styles of writing

Present tense – *are*

Impersonal language – note the use of general terms, e.g.
children, neighbourhoods, local authorities, community life

Passives –

If <u>they are denied</u> a role in community life, young people will continue to be disillusioned with, and dismissive of, politics, government and the democratic process.

The quality and effectiveness of local councils' involvement of children and young people <u>should be assessed</u> against their duty to consult with local residents and other providers of local services.

Complex sentences –

Fear of violence and crime, based on the grim reality of bullying at school and assaults in the community, concern about drugs and the danger of traffic are key factors in this change.

Children need to be able to participate in decisions made about their own environment, to contribute towards plans for safe housing, traffic-free streets, play and leisure facilities, accessible shops and safe open spaces.

Complex sentences (5)

The purpose of this unit is to experiment with complex sentences. Pupils will write a story, using a range of sentence types for maximum impact.

NLS coverage

Key objective

SL 4 To secure control of complex sentences, understanding how clauses can be manipulated to achieve different effects

Learned through:

TL Reading comprehension and writing composition
5, 6, 12 To compare and contrast the work of a single writer; to look at connections and contrasts in the work of different writers; to compare texts in writing, drawing out: their different styles and preoccupations, their strengths and weaknesses, their different values and appeal to a reader
14 To write an extended story, worked on over time on a theme identified in reading

Assessment criteria

SL By the end of this unit, pupils should be able to identify different types of complex sentence; identify the impact of different sentence structures; use a range of sentences to create impact in their writing.

TL Writing composition
Children should be able to write a longer narrative, borrowing/incorporating features from the styles of other writers.

Session 1

You will need OHT 23 and PCM 23A.

Shared reading

1 Explain that you will be looking at two pieces of writing about the same event – the final game in the 1988–9 football season. This was a historic match between Liverpool and Arsenal. If Liverpool won, drew or even lost 1–0, they would win the Championship; if Arsenal won 2–0 or more, they would win the Championship. Discuss what the atmosphere might have been like. How would the fans have been feeling? How about the players?

2 Read the text through to the class. Can they identify a viewpoint? Does the writer sympathize with one team? If so, what is it that suggests this bias to them? Look for the clues.

Sentence level work

1 Explain to pupils that you will be looking at how the writer has used different sentence structures to

good effect. Begin by looking at the first sentence. What effect does this have? Now look at the next few sentences. What do pupils notice about these sentences? The first has one clause and six words. Pupils should see that the sentences get longer and more complex. Note how this adds to the build-up of excitement in the paragraph. There are three other short sentences. Can pupils locate them? Discuss the reasons for their brevity, and why the final sentence is a very short one too.

2 Now look at the more complex sentences. Consider how they have been put together, e.g.
Grobbelaar made no effort to save it; the linesman raised a flag, but the referee reckoned Alan Smith had touched the ball before it went over the line.
Note how there are three points of information. The first two clauses are linked by a semi-colon: this is a list of points in support of one side of the argument. The other point – the referee's decision – is linked with the contrastive connective *but*.

3 Use this sentence as a model for other sentences. For example:
The doll had never been advertised on TV; it looked really cheap, but my little sister thought it was the cutest toy she had ever seen.

Independent activities

1 Direct pupils to PCM 23A which has the next paragraph from the same text but with clauses separated and jumbled up. Pupils, individually or in a guided group, should cut the text into strips and reconstruct it as a paragraph. They are prompted to use cues such as sentence length and punctuation.

2 Pupils who finish early may compose a paragraph to precede the OHT text. This should focus on the atmosphere in the stadium before the match.

Plenary

Pupils who have completed the task read out their opening paragraphs. Discuss the way in which these fit what follows. Which is the 'best fit', and why?

Session 2

You will need pupils' book 4, Unit 23, pages 54–5, and PCM 23B.

Shared reading

1 During this session, pupils will be reading a different version of the same event. Ask them to predict the viewpoint from which this may be written. What differences do they expect, and why?

2 Allow pupils five minutes to read the text. Plot the writer's emotions during the time period covered by the text. Do this as a simple line graph. The text covers about 45 minutes, from the first Arsenal goal to the final whistle. Discuss the way in which the passage of time is treated – why there is very close detail on some sections, but no detail at all for about 35 minutes of a crucial football match.

3 Look closely at the language Nick Hornby uses to convey his changing emotions.

Sentence level work

1 Consider Nick Hornby's writing style. Invite pupils to comment on anything they have noted. Draw attention to sentence length. Is it regular? Is there any variation? Invite pupils to highlight the two longest sentences in one colour, and the two shortest sentences in another colour. Discuss their position in the text, and the impact of short and long sentences. Note how complex sentences allow the writer to link ideas and events in different ways, while shorter sentences in the midst of longer sentences have impact.

2 Discuss the impact of breaking longer sentences down into shorter sentences.

3 Use Hornby's longer sentences as a model for other sentences, for example:
   – *I could find it in me to forgive them for coming so close and blowing it: they were young, and they'd had a fantastic season and as a supporter you cannot really ask for more than that.*
   – *He congratulated the children: they had worked hard and they'd collected lots of cards and as a teacher you have to encourage enthusiasm.*

4 Look at other sentences which could be used as models. Encourage children to write sentences of their own. Circulate, encouraging pupils and helping them to move forward.

5 Collect examples, and focus on punctuation.

Independent activities

Children complete questions A and B in the pupils' book. Use PCM 23B as an extension activity or for homework.

Plenary

1 Ask pupils to comment on the impact of changing the sentences. What were the key effects? Did the shorter sentences build up tension as well?

2 Work with one of the 'favourite' sentences from PCM 23B. Discuss which words were changed.

3 Before undertaking the writing task in Session 3, it will be important for pupils to watch, listen to or read about an exciting sporting event. Identify an appropriate focus for the writing, so that pupils can prepare for writing.

Session 3

You will need pupils' book 4, Unit 23, pages 54–5, and the Reminder Sheet.

Shared writing

1 Explain to pupils that you will be writing about the event which has been selected. List the key incidents/parts of the event.

2 Plot the level of excitement during the course of the event. Use this to help you select incidents to include in the recount – highlight these. Remind pupils that it is not necessary to cover everything that happened – Nick Hornby left out about 90% of the action in the second half of the Liverpool–Arsenal game.

3 Revisit key elements of Hornby's style, e.g. complex sentences to link ideas and build up excitement.

Write together

Begin on the first paragraph of the recount. Experiment with creating longer sentences, varying the sequence of the clauses. Remember to be explicit about the punctuation of these sentences.

Independent writing activity

Pupils begin on their own versions. Work with a group who need support or additional challenge.

Plenary

Pupils work in small groups to select features of initial attempts which are reminiscent of Hornby's style for sharing with the rest of the class.

Session 4

You will need pupils' book 4, Unit 23, pages 54–5, and the Reminder Sheet.

Shared writing

Continue writing.

Write together

Discuss ideas for sentences. Ask pupils to write their own versions and discuss in pairs before contributing them. Use this strategy three times at most – for sentences of different lengths. Rehearse sentences orally. Ask pupils to contribute to this.

Independent writing activity

Pupils complete the writing.

Plenary

1 Focus on the extent to which pupils' writing matches Hornby's style. Invite successful pupils to contribute – refer back to the model text.

2 List what has been learned about writing recounts, and whether any of this could be transferred to writing narrative with imaginative content (story!). Pupils should select one of these ideas as a focus for their next piece of writing.

Assessment

Pupils should be able to:
- identify complex sentences, and explain writers' choice of using them
- compose a range of sentences on the same idea, and select the best for the purpose
- punctuate complex sentences accurately.

Model answers

Pupils' book 4 ☐ A

1 This match will decide who wins the Championship.

2 Answers will vary. He was probably very nervous.

3 Answers will vary. Hope and fear are likely to figure!

4 There is no right answer here – pupils should give evidence/explanation for their choice.

5 Pupils should understand that previous years when Arsenal had won nothing were wiped out in Hornby's mind.

Pupils' book 4 ☐ B

6 Answers will vary.

7 Variety of sentence length and complexity; he writes only about important parts of the match; first person; emotional.

☐23A   Complex sentences (5)

Rarely has Anfield looked so dejected.
Fans shook their heads in disbelief,
there was a stunned silence from the Kop,
though they generously applauded Arsenal as they lifted the trophy.
Thousands poured out of Anfield into the night air,
barely a word being spoken,
wandering off to their cars and buses in disbelief at what they had just seen.
They have a word for it in Liverpool.
Gobsmacked.

☐23B   Complex sentences (5)
Answers will vary.

Jigsaw

This is the next paragraph from the recount of the Liverpool–Arsenal match. The clauses have been jumbled up. Cut the text into strips, then try to rebuild the paragraph.

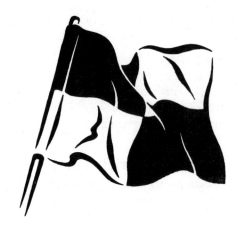

Remember to look at:
- punctuation
- sentence length – especially how the writer uses short sentences for effect at the beginning and end of the paragraph.

---

there was a stunned silence from the Kop,

Gobsmacked.

Fans shook their heads in disbelief,

Thousands poured out of Anfield into the night air,

Rarely has Anfield looked so dejected.

---

barely a word being spoken,

---

though they generously applauded Arsenal as they lifted the trophy.

They have a word for it in Liverpool.

---

wandering off to their cars and buses in disbelief at what they had just seen.

Sentences from *The Hamlyn Illustrated History of Liverpool* by Stephen Kelly (Hamlyn, 1996)

Here is a sentence from Nick Hornby's account of the Liverpool vs Arsenal match. Use this sentence as a model for other sentences. There are ideas for other sentences below, but you can always use your own. See how much you can use this sentence to create others.

> ## Liverpool vs Arsenal
>
> *I got excited when we scored right at the beginning of the second half, and I got excited again about ten minutes from time, when Thomas had a clear chance and hit it straight at Grobbelaar, but Liverpool seemed to be growing stronger and to be creating chances at the end, and finally, with the clock in the corner of the TV screen showing that the ninety minutes had passed, I got ready to muster a brave smile for a brave team.*

Ideas:

- a football match
- a quiz show / game show
- a race
- waiting for guests to arrive at a party.

When you have finished, highlight your favourite sentence to share with other pupils.

_____

_____

_____

_____

_____

_____

_____

_____

Sentence from *Fever Pitch* by Nick Hornby (Victor Gollancz, 1992), copyright © Nick Hornby 1992, reprinted by permission of The Penguin Group UK.

Sentence structure

Writers use different sentence structures to good effect.

They vary sentence length, sometimes using short sentences which stand out, and sometimes longer, compound or complex sentences which link ideas.

For example, a short sentence might be:
It was like a bad dream.
Liverpool had been denied the Double.

An example of a more complicated sentence might be:
Grobbelaar made no effort to save it; the linesman raised a flag, but the referee reckoned Alan Smith had touched it before it went over the line.

You can use this sentence as a model for other sentences. For example:
The doll had never been advertised on TV; it looked really cheap, but my little sister thought it was the cutest toy she had ever seen.

Punctuation

It is important to look at punctuation in longer sentences as this will help readers work out how ideas are linked. Writers use commas and colons inside sentences to help readers. For example:
I could find it in me to forgive them for coming so close and blowing it: they were young, and they'd had a fantastic season and as a supporter you cannot really ask for more than that.

Developing a theme

The purpose of this unit is to investigate writers' use of language, and how they use language to develop their themes.

NLS coverage

Key objective

SL **2** To conduct detailed language investigations through interviews, research and reading, e.g. of proverbs, language change over time, dialect, study of headlines

Learned through:

TL **Reading comprehension and writing composition**
2 To discuss how linked poems relate to one another by themes, format and repetition, e.g. cycle of poems about the seasons
3 To describe and evaluate the style of an individual poet
4 To comment critically on the overall impact of a poem, showing how language and themes have been developed
13 To write a sequence of poems linked by theme or form, e.g. a haiku calendar

Assessment criteria

SL By the end of this unit, pupils should be able to identify features of language which characterize particular writers.

TL **Writing composition**
Children should be able to develop a theme in the style of an author, using typical structures and language.

Session 1

You will need OHT 24 and PCM 24A.

Shared reading

1 Explain that you will be reading two poems over the next sessions. The first is about old age. Ask pupils what they expect. Offer team points to pupils who can offer any words (apart from those on the list of high frequency words!) which are in the poem.

2 Display and read OHT 24. Invite pupils to discuss the poem. What sort of attitudes does the writer have to ageing? Pupils should refer to the text when expressing these opinions – they should demonstrate that they can find evidence to support their opinions.

3 Invite pupils to reread the poem, practising reading aloud using appropriate expression. Discuss readings by two or three pupils – how have they expressed the feelings of the poet, and conveyed this to listeners?

Sentence level work

1 Consider the language in the poem. Do pupils notice anything about sentences and how they start? Draw attention to the long compound sentences which start *I shall...* Would children have written it this way, or would they have written *I will...*? This is an area of change in language. 'Sticklers' might say that the form *shall* should be used for the first person future, while *will* is used for the second and third persons (*I shall go / you will go*). *Shall* is also used in tag questions, e.g. *I'll go, shall I?* Some people also use *shall* to signal intent – that someone is choosing to do something, maybe against the odds, e.g. *I shall go to the ball.* Discuss with pupils what they think might be the case here. Experiment with using *shall* in sentences. (Explain that the word *shall* has almost disappeared from American and Australian English.)

2 Discuss the use of *shall not / shan't* – often associated with the language of toddlers! Do pupils think either of these is used very much nowadays?

3 Draw pupils' attention to the way the writer uses different verb forms in other verses, e.g. *you can, we must.* How does that help the poem? What does

that say about how the writer views adulthood? Do you think she likes setting a good example? Do you think she looks forward to behaving badly? She never says, so there are no clear answers – but the way she uses her verbs gives us some clues.

Independent activities

Pupils complete PCM 24A which allows them to investigate the use of the word *shall*.

Plenary

1   Discuss what pupils found. Was one type of usage more common than another? Did the word occur in certain types of text? Did usage vary between writers?

2   End the lesson with a discussion about why pupils think the word is slowly disappearing.

Session 2

You will need pupils' book 4, Unit 24, pages 56–7, PCM 24B, and the Reminder Sheet.

Shared reading

1   Explain that the text you are going to read is a song lyric, but that the layout and other features are very similar to a poem. Explain that this is a Beatles song, written by John Lennon and Paul McCartney. Ask pupils to turn to page 56 in the pupils' book. You could either read the song, or play a version of it to the pupils.

2   How did the song make pupils feel? How did it do that? Was it lyrics, music or a combination?

3   Discuss the character of Eleanor Rigby. Plot out what she does each day – ask pupils to refer to the text to explain their suggestions. For example, she might go to church. Why would she do that? There will probably be more than one reason.

4   Why is the song called *Eleanor Rigby*, when there are two main characters?

Sentence level work

1   Focus on the refrain, and look at how the writers have used language to create particular effects.

2   For example, why do you think they have referred to <u>*all*</u> *the lonely people*? The word *all* has a special meaning here. Discuss the literal meaning of the word, and contrast it to the way it is used here. It

may be useful to think of examples of times when other people may use this structure, for example:
Listen to all those birds.
Look at all those dirty clothes on the floor.
Note that these are both commands – they draw the listeners' attention, and the use of *all* exaggerates. Encourage children to think of other ways of using *all* so that it exaggerates something.

3   Ask children to think of other words which are often used, but not in their literal sense, or used for emphasis. Many of these are 'over-used'. They may suggest: *really/never/actually*. Discuss how they might be used, and why. Are pupils aware of using any words in this way? Would they be more likely to use them in speech or in writing? Discuss how we use exaggeration more in informal situations with people we know than when talking to or writing for people we do not know.

4   There are other ways of emphasizing something, for example using the verb *do* as in *I did see a flying saucer*; using the word *it* as in *it was a flying saucer I saw*; and using pronouns *I saw the flying saucer myself*. Discuss these with pupils.

Independent activities

Children complete questions A and B in the pupils' book. Pupils may go on to complete PCM 24B, which is an investigation similar to PCM 24A, and use the Reminder Sheet to help them.

Plenary

Discuss pupils' work on emphasis.

Session 3

You will need pupils' book 4, Unit 24, pages 56–7, and the Reminder Sheet.

Shared writing

1   Look back at 'Eleanor Rigby'. Reread, or listen to the song again. Explain that you will be using this as a model for a poem about another human state. Begin by selecting this. Pupils can choose any emotion – it may be more comfortable to look at something neutral such as *busy*.

2   First look at the verse structure. Notice that each verse begins with a name, then describes an activity, then another activity.

Write together

1 Begin to write the first verse as a class. Model the selection of appropriate detail, and look at how this can add emphasis. Choice of names is also important – no names of pupils in the school; ordinary names, or names that suggest the age or occupation of the individual would be appropriate.

2 Draw pupils' attention to the way the song is written in the present tense. Why is this effective? Experiment with different tenses as you write. Discuss the best choice.

3 Consider the refrain. It would be possible to simply swap *busy* for *lonely*. Will this work? You could use this as a 'stopgap' – it can be changed later.

4 Continue writing verses, as time allows. Note how Lennon and McCartney link their two characters through the idea of the church, but never describe them meeting. Could a similar device be used here?

Independent writing activity

Pupils embark on their own poem. They should select their own topic, and use a similar structure.

Plenary

Pupils read poems to each other in pairs, and give advice. Draw the class together for the final five minutes, and ask if any pupils have received really useful advice. They could share that with the rest of the class.

Session 4

You will need pupils' book 4, Unit 24, pages 56–7, and the Reminder Sheet.

Shared writing

Revise the poem written on the previous occasion. Remind pupils of the need to return to texts before publishing so that they can be improved.

Write together

1 Model use of editing marks as you write; take suggestions from pupils about what to change. Make sure that you reread frequently – poems are written to be read aloud. Check that it sounds right, that the rhythm and rhyme – if any – are working.

2 Finish the poem by revisiting the refrains and checking that they work.

Independent writing activity

Pupils complete their own poems.

Plenary

Pupils should read their completed poems aloud. Those pupils like best may be selected for sharing at assembly.

Assessment

Pupils should be able to:
• understand that language changes over time
• understand that individuals vary in their use of language
• use the verb *shall*
• use a range of strategies for emphasis.

Model answers

Pupils' book 4 ☐ **A**

1 Answers will vary. It is likely she is elderly.

2 Pupils may feel this refers to use of make-up, or that she makes a definite effort to arrange her features when she leaves the house.

3 This means that no-one will remember her or use her name again; it also suggests she had no children.

4 Answers will vary. He may feel sad, because she was one of the few people he saw in church regularly. Her fate may remind him of his own loneliness.

5 Answers will vary.

Pupils' book 4 ☐ **B**

6 *all* is used literally in the second sentence.

7 Answers will vary.

☐ **24A and 24B** 🖵

Answers will vary. Check that pupils have understood these features.

24A Shall or will?

Look through your reading books to find some examples of where writers have used the word 'shall'. Decide why they have used it, and fill in the table.

First person future	Tag question	Intent	Other

Once you have finished, make a note of anything else you notice, for example, was one type of usage more common than another; did the word occur in certain types of text?

24ʙ Emphasis

Look for examples of emphasis in reading books.

Sample (write out example)	Source – who wrote it?	Form – what sort is it?	Effect – does it work?

24 *Developing a theme*

Shall or will?

This is an area of change in language. 'Sticklers' might say that the form *shall* should be used:

- for the first person future, while *will* is used for the second and third persons (*I shall go / you will go*).
- in tag questions, e.g. *I'll go, shall I?*
- to signal intent – that someone is choosing to do something, maybe against the odds, e.g. *I shall go to the ball.*

Emphasis

Writers and speakers often use words to add emphasis, for example *all*. Not all these words are used *literally*. You could use:

- *really*
- *truly*
- *extremely*
- *actually*
- *literally*.

There are other ways of emphasizing something, for example:

- using the verb *do*, as in *I <u>did</u> see a flying saucer.*
- using the word *it*, as in *<u>it</u> was a flying saucer I saw.*
- using pronouns, as in *I saw the flying saucer <u>myself</u>.*

Developing a style

The purpose of this unit is to investigate language variation; how individual writers bring their own style, and the impact this can have on readers. Pupils will write interview questions and a persuasive piece.

NLS coverage

Key objective

SL 2 To conduct detailed language investigations through interviews, research and reading, e.g. of proverbs, language change over time, dialect, study of headlines

Learned through:

TL **Reading comprehension and writing composition**
1 To describe and evaluate the style of an individual writer
7 To annotate passages in detail in response to specific questions
8 To use a reading journal effectively to raise and refine personal responses to a text and prepare for discussion
9, 10, 11 To write summaries of texts, deciding on priorities relevant to purpose; to write a brief synopsis of a text, e.g. for a back cover blurb; to write a brief helpful review tailored for real audiences

Assessment criteria

SL By the end of this unit, pupils should be able to identify language features of different speakers and writers; understand differences between written speech and writing.

TL **Writing composition**
Children should be able to write in the style of an author, using typical structures and language.

Session 1

You will need OHT 25 and PCM 25A.

Shared reading

1 Explain to pupils that you will be reading two texts about zoos. Ask whether pupils have been to zoos, and whether or not they enjoyed the experience.

2 Display the OHT text and read it aloud to pupils. It is by a twelve-year-old boy. (You will need to practise it first so that it sounds like natural language.) Do pupils think the boy interviewed liked the zoo? Keep this brief – it should not become a debate on zoos.

3 Go through the text, noting the main points. It may be helpful to underline/highlight key ideas.

4 Notice the structure of the text. Aidan begins by talking about his views on the positive aspects of zoos. He then gives an example of what he likes about zoos. In the final paragraph there is a mix of positive and negative points.

Sentence level work

1 Ask pupils what they noticed about the reading. They should have noticed that it was a transcription of an interview, or discussion. Ask them to identify the clues to this. They should refer to informal language structure, oral grammar (*there's*), use of second person (*don't you*), repetition of words that fill gaps (*like*) in the way that *erm* does.

2 Discuss they way the writer has done the transcription. What has been added? Consider: spelling/punctuation/paragraphing.

3 Remind children that spoken language varies considerably, in many ways: accent is perhaps the most obvious way, but there are also other

differences. Ask pupils if they can guess where Aidan lives (North West England). Gather clues to this (e.g. use of *there's*, *like*, *mind*). To emphasize this point, ask pupils to transform the text into another dialect. It may be easiest to start with something completely different, for example standard English or US English.

4 Beginning with the first paragraph, ask pupils to transform the language into the identified version. Ask them to think of how they know what they are doing – for example, for US English they may be drawing on experience from television.

Independent activities

Pupils use PCM 25A to draft a version of the same ideas using a different dialect of English. When they have completed the text they should practise reading it aloud. At this point, they can introduce accent.

Plenary

1 Select pupils to read aloud from their version of the text. Can other pupils identify the dialect? Try to probe beyond accent in looking for identification.

2 Revisit Aidan's material. Would he have convinced you, if he were trying to persuade you? Do you think he will ever change his mind about zoos? What makes you think that? Would you use Aidan as a speaker if you were organizing an event to support zoos?

Session 2

Shared writing

1 Explain that you will be investigating language through interviewing different people about their opinions on zoos. The aim of the exercise is to generate as much language difference as possible between two 'types' of people. Ask children to suggest pairs of people who might generate a lot of contrast – for example, think of differences related to gender/age/region. Discuss the possible variations – pupils may suggest variation in vocabulary, sentence structure and other characteristics such as 'place holders' – phrases people pepper throughout their speech, such as *erm*. Pupils decide which direction the investigation will take. They all select an appropriate interviewee so that there is a balance.

2 In order to make this fair, it will be important to ask both 'types' of interviewee the same questions.

Write together

As a class, write questions for the interviews. Demonstrate writing questions that do not lead the interviewee one way or another. Write at least two questions as a class.

Independent writing activity

Pupils work in pairs to compose the remaining questions. Once finished, they should select the two questions they feel are most important.

Plenary

Gather pupils' questions – are there any questions on which pupils agree? Build up a class list of questions. Check that the questions have been composed so that they are not leading. Pupils will conduct and record interviews as homework.

Session 3

You will need the pupils' completed interviews

Shared reading

1 Divide the class in half – according to 'type' of interviewee. Explain that they should work in groups to look for similarities and differences in terms of language. Allow 10 minutes for this. Bring the class back together. Begin listing the features of the groups.

2 Once the features are listed, discuss similarities and differences. Are differences more or less than had been expected? Find examples.

Independent activity

Pupils write up their findings.

Plenary

Explain that in the next session you will be looking at the individual style of one writer. Ask pupils to think of writers they like, and why.

Session 4

You will need pupils' book 4, Unit 25,
pages 58–9, PCM 25B, and the Reminder Sheet.

Shared reading

1 Today, pupils will be reading another text about the moral issues surrounding zoos. This is an extract from a much longer article – and is the first part of that article. It is very different in tone from the other piece. Look at the way Stephen Fry has built up his argument. Why has he looked at other issues? Pupils should see that he has selected issues that were not issues for a long time – the situations were accepted and acceptable, but are not now.

2 Ask pupils whether they think this is a good way of arguing the case. Why?

Sentence level work

1 Ask pupils if they notice anything unusual about Fry's writing. Explore the language he has used. Ask pupils to identify anything they like about it. Do they all feel the same about it?

2 It is important not to dissect the language so that it loses its appeal – a difficult balance to strike!

3 Explain to pupils that they will be writing an argument in favour of or against zoos. They have covered a lot of material in this area over the past few sessions, and should be familiar with the structure of persuasive pieces. PCM 25B offers a planning sheet.

Independent activities

Pupils plan their persuasive piece. If they are happy with the plan, they may begin to write.

Plenary

Invite pupils to share their ideas so far. Focus on opening paragraphs; invite comments from other pupils. Writing can be completed for homework or in a later session.

Assessment

Pupils should be able to understand that writers and speakers use individual habits; identify similarities and differences between language users; write persuasively.

Model answers

Pupils' book 4 ◺ A

1 He enjoyed them when he was a little boy, but seems less sure now.
2 He refers to slavery and votes for women.
3 He links them because slavery and women not having a vote were once acceptable in Britain, and are now unacceptable. He suggests that this might in the future be true for zoos.
4 To persuade people to his point of view.
5 Pupils will probably feel that he is writing for adults. His vocabulary and sentence structure are mostly complex; his use of humour and wordplay will be better understood by adults than most children.

Pupils' book 4 ◺ B

6 Answers will vary.
7 Answers will vary.

◺ 25A and 25B ▯

Answers will vary.

Draft a version of Aidan's ideas using a different dialect of English.

When you have completed your text, practise reading it aloud. Try using the appropriate accent.

Interview with Aidan

I like zoos, me. We go to Chester – it's been on the telly and everything. There's lots of different species there, loads of them are dying out in the wild. The zoo, like, helps save them from going extinct. They breed them and swap with other zoos all over the world. I think that's a good thing.

My best ones are the lions and tigers – they're just massive! Sometimes, though, they just lie down. They do in the wild, like, but you want to see them do something, don't you?

Mum says zoos are better now than what they were when she was my age, because they don't have cages now, they have enclosures, and they, like, try to make it homely for the animals. You've got to feel sorry for some of the animals, mind. That tiger just goes up and down, up and down. I don't know what the animals feel like in the winter. They mostly come from Africa and India, and I don't think it gets that cold over there.

_____

_____

_____

_____

_____

_____

_____

_____

Use this frame to plan your piece of persuasive writing.

Title	
Opening paragraph	
First point	
Second point	
Conclusion	

25 *Developing a style*

Writing and speaking are very different. Even if the same person is trying to communicate the same message, they will use different language depending on whether they are writing or speaking.

Speaking

In speaking, you will probably find:

- informal language structure
- oral grammar (*them is*)
- use of second person (*don't you*)
- repetition of words that fill gaps (*like*) in the way *erm* does.

Most people talk with an accent, which cannot be detected in their writing.

Most people use <u>dialect</u> when talking.

Writing

Writers develop their own special style. For example, Stephen Fry uses very unusual images. His writing is easy to distinguish. How could you develop your own personal style?

When you are writing, think about:

- the words and phrases you choose – are they different from the ones other people might use?
- sentence structure – do you vary sentences or do you always use the same sort of sentence?
- the <u>voice</u> you adopt – do you prefer to address readers directly or do you tend to be more formal in your writing?

The more writing you do, for different situations and different readers, the more your own personal style will develop. Enjoy your writing!